LIBERTY
ITS USE AND ABUSE

―――

VOLUME I

―――

BASIC PRINCIPLES
OF ETHICS

By IGNATIUS W. COX, S.J., Ph.D.

FORDHAM UNIVERSITY PRESS
NEW YORK

BJ 1249
C 87
V. 1
co, 3

COPYRIGHT, 1936, BY
Fordham University Press

PRINTED IN THE UNITED STATES OF AMERICA

95384

CONTENTS

INTRODUCTION

IT is perfectly obvious to-day that the so-called Liberals, as a group, bear the air of an army beating a quick retreat, if not of an army completely defeated. By Liberals, of course, I mean those individuals and those organizations which were attacked as usurping the name of liberty by Leo XIII in his brilliant encyclical, "On Human Liberty." "What Naturalists or Rationalists aim at in philosophy, that the supporters of Liberalism, carrying out the principles laid down by Naturalism, are attempting in the domain of morality and politics. The fundamental doctrine of Rationalism is the supremacy of the human reason, which, refusing due submission to the Divine and eternal reason, proclaims its own independence, and constitutes itself the supreme principle and source and judge of truth. Hence these followers of Liberalism deny the existence of any Divine authority to which obedience is due, and proclaim that every man is a law to himself; from which arises that ethical system which they style *independent morality,* and which, under the *guise* of liberty, exonerates man from any obedience to the commands of God, and substitutes a boundless license. The end of all this it is not difficult to foresee, especially when society is in question. For, when once man is firmly persuaded that he is subject to no one, it follows that the efficient cause of the unity of civil society is not to be sought in any principle external to man, or superior to him, but simply in the free will of individuals; that the authority in the State comes from the people only; and that, just as every man's individual reason is his only rule of life, so the collective reason of the community should be the supreme guide in the management of all public affairs. Hence the doctrine of the supremacy of the greater number, and that all right and all duty reside in the majority. But, from what has been said, it is clear that all this is in contradiction to reason."

The doctrines of "Liberalism," attacked by Leo XIII in 1888, have at last reached their logical conclusion. The evidence for this lies all around us. Such liberty unrestrained by law, which ultimately proceeds from the Supreme Lawgiver, God, has eventuated in *license.* Disintegralism has become the characteristic of modern life in morals, in science, in education, in government, and in international relationships. The reaction to this disintegralism, inimical as it is to human life and well-being, shows itself in the decline of democracy and in the advent of dictatorships. The vaunted liberty which was to make us free has eventuated in a more galling servitude to man's lower nature, especially to sex on the one hand, and to autocratic political power on the other.

It is only the truth which can make us free and the truth is that liberty unchecked by law, the Natural Law of God and human law in accordance with the law of God, leads to *license* and thence to servitude. Correct principles with regard to "Liberty, Its Use and Abuse," are set forth here as the contribution of the *"Philosophia Perennis"* for the restoration of human liberty to its proper place in the affairs of men.

This little book is dedicated to my beloved pupils, past, present and future, in the hope that they will study diligently and absorb deeply the principles herein set forth. Thus they will equip themselves to be leaders in a world which above all needs leaders, to save man's liberty from the disastrous materialistic principles which have worked its ruin and above all to save American liberty from the dangers that assault it on every side.

No claim is made to originality in the pages which follow. I have more than often, by mere translation, followed in the footsteps of my own brilliant Professor of Ethics, Timothy J. Brosnahan, S.J. I have supplemented his rich learning, wherever I found it convenient, by the ethical writings of Charles W. Macksey, S.J., of the Gregorian University at Rome; and of Charles Lamb, S.J., of Woodstock College, Maryland. The writings of the distinguished Jesuit ethicians, Victor Cathrein, S.J., of Valkenburgh, in Holland; Joseph Donat, S.J., of Innsbruck, in Austria; and Marcellus Nivard, S.J., of the French Scholasticate of the Society of Jesus, on the island of Jersey in England, have frequently been used, sometimes by mere translation. All this is not to say that I am not indebted to the works of other celebrated ethicians whose writings both in English, in Latin, and in the vernacular of their native lands are familiar to students of Scholàstic Ethics.

The topics for discussion which are presented at the end of chapters or theses are so devised that their answers bring out the essential points to be assimilated. Students are earnestly advised to avail themselves of the list of readings presented at the end of each chapter, but only after they have absorbed the contents of that chapter.

IGNATIUS W. COX, S.J., PH.D.,
Professor of Ethics,
Fordham University.

Feast of the Assumption
of Our Blessed Lady,
August 15, 1936.

CHAPTER I

The Definition of Ethics

1. Ethics is the practical natural science directive of the right use of human liberty.

Human liberty is that property of the will in virtue of which the will has the power to act or not to act, to act in one way or to act in another, when all the elements for the proper determination of itself are present. This freedom is called freedom of choice or simply free will and is liberty with regard either to the contradictory or to the contrary. The exercise of liberty, viz., a free act of the will, is called *human conduct* or *volitional activity,* to distinguish it from all other activity in the visible universe.

The right use—these words imply that, although man has physical liberty of choice in some of his activities, nevertheless, not all use of human liberty is a right use of it. All men agree that the exercise of human liberty is in some cases *right* and *good,* in other cases *wrong* and *bad.* This distinction between right and wrong, good and bad in human conduct is universally admitted. Different reasons for the distinction are assigned by different systems of ethics. The fact of the distinction which man makes between right and wrong, good and bad in human conduct is called the *Ethical Fact.* This may be described as follows: "All men judge that there is a difference between right and wrong, good and bad in man's free activity. In consequence, therefore, they judge that there are some free actions which man *ought* not to elicit and some which he *ought* to elicit." In this Ethical Fact, which represents a universal judgment of the race, there are three elements which the ethician must investigate and validate. First, is it true that some free actions are right and good, some wrong and evil? Secondly, what is it that makes some free acts of the will right and good, others wrong and evil? Thirdly, is there an obligation on man's will to elicit right and good free actions, and to refrain from wrong and evil free actions? This obligation is expressed by the term *oughtness* or *duty,* i.e., *ought man,* or has man the duty to elicit right and good free acts of the will and similarly to omit wrong and evil free acts of the will? The term *ought* evidently contains two elements, viz., that the free action in question is good and that there is an obligation to elicit it. Likewise the term *ought not* contains two elements, viz., that the free action in question is evil and that there is an obligation not to elicit it. Basic Ethics is largely concerned with these three major questions and the subsidiary ones connected with them.

1

A *science*—we say that Ethics is a science. A science is any body of truths, co-ordinated under principles by which they are explained and methodically formulated into a system. There can be a science of truths which are revealed by God, hence a science of supernatural truths. Ethics is a science of natural truths, viz., truths attained solely by the light of natural reason. A science may be either speculative or practical, according as its aim is primarily knowledge or primarily action. Ethics, aiming to direct man in the use of his prerogative of liberty, is a practical science.

TOPICS FOR DISCUSSION

1. What is the definition of Ethics?

2. What do you mean by human liberty?

3. Why do you say that liberty is a property of the will alone?

4. Does liberty essentially consist in the power to choose either of two contradictories?

5. What do you mean by the clause, "When all the elements for a *proper* determination of itself are present?"

6. What is the technical name for the exercise of human liberty?

7. Does this technical name distinguish the exercise of liberty from all other activity in the visible universe?

8. What is the implication in the phrase, "A right use of human liberty?"

9. Do all agree that some exercise of human liberty is right and good, other exercise wrong and evil?

10. In what phrase is the universal admission of a distinction between good and evil in human conduct summed up?

11. State the Ethical Fact.

12. Do all agree in the explanation of the Ethical Fact?

13. Do we presuppose the truth of the judgments contained in the Ethical Fact?

14. What are the three elements in the Ethical Fact which it is the task of the ethician to investigate?

15. What are the elements contained in the term, *ought?*

16. What is a science?

17. Is there a distinction between natural and supernatural science?

18. Is Ethics a supernatural science?

19. What is the distinction between speculative and practical science?

20. Is Ethics a practical science? Why?

READINGS FOR CHAPTER I*

Catholic Encyclopedia, "Ethics," vol. v, p. 556; "Morality," vol. x, p. 559; "Free Will," vol. vi, p. 259.

Rickaby, *Political and Moral Essays,* chap. vi, "Morality without Free Will," p. 249.

Nivard, Introduction, *Vues Synthetiques Sur le Problème Moral* (in French).

Ross, Introduction, chap. i.

Theses in General Ethics, thesis i.

Moore, Preliminary Notions, pp. 1-10.

Leibell, Introduction, pp. 1-19.

Cronin, chap. i, pp. 1-21.

Donat, *Freedom of Science,* 1st sect., pp. 3-59.

Belloc, the whole book.

---

* Titles, names of authors, and publishers of the books from which these readings are recommended will be found on pp. 152 and 153.

CHAPTER II

The General and Particular Objects of Ethics

2. A science is a systematized body of truths with a proper subject-matter and a particular view-point. The proper subject-matter of Ethics is *exercised liberty* or *human conduct* or *volitional activity*. The particular view-point of Ethics with regard to this subject-matter is *oughtness* or *duty,* viz., the duty of eliciting certain volitional acts and the duty of avoiding others. We shall first consider the elements constituting *human conduct* or *volitional activity,* then the meaning of the terms, *ought* or *duty.*

3. The General Object of Ethics.

A. The Nature of Volitional Acts.

Human conduct or volitional activity is an act which proceeds from deliberate reason and free will. Antecedently to the exercise of free will, it is necessary for the intellect to weigh the reasons for and against a certain line of conduct. After the deliberation of the intellect, the will chooses which course to follow. This is an exercise of human liberty. Only such an exercise of the will is human conduct or volitional activity, and only such is the proper subject-matter of Ethics.

> **N.B.**—The external act, e.g., walking, riding, etc., is not in itself free. It is *denominated* free because it *depends upon* the free choice of the will. Ethics is principally engaged in considering the act of the will itself, for in many cases no external activity follows. The external act is called a *commanded* act of the will; the act of the will itself is called an *elicited* act, inasmuch as it is completed in the faculty which causes it.

It is clear, then, that acts which are not distinctive of man as an intelligent being, e.g., circulation of the blood, are not volitional acts, hence not the proper subject-matter of Ethics. It is also evident that voluntary but necessary acts are not volitional acts, because the element of freedom is not present.

B. The Division of Volitional Acts.

Volitional acts are *perfect* or *imperfect,* according to the perfection or imperfection of the deliberation and according to the perfection or imperfection of the consent of the will.

Volitional acts are *direct* or *indirect*. A directly volitional act terminates in an object which is willed as *an end* or as *a means to an end*. An indirectly volitional act terminates in an object which is not willed as *an end* or as *a means to an end,* but which is necessarily connected with the object of a direct volitional act.

Volitional acts are also *actual, virtual, habitual* or *interpretative.* This division of conduct will be treated later on in this work.

C. Circumstances Affecting Volitional Acts.

There are three circumstances which affect the volitional character of conduct. Since a volitional act proceeds from deliberate reason and free will, any circumstance which affects either knowledge, deliberation or freedom, will likewise affect the volitional character of the act. These three circumstances are *ignorance, concupiscence* and *fear.*

Ignorance is the absence of knowledge in one who has the faculty of knowing. It can be *ignorance of law,* or *ignorance of fact.* Ignorance modifies the volitional character of an act by affecting the knowledge necessary for true volition.

Ignorance of *Law* is absence of knowledge of the law's existence or of the law's comprehension of this particular case.

Ignorance of *fact* is the absence of knowledge of either the substance or of some circumstance of the thing wished or to be done. For example: One who makes a contract with a demented person, not knowing that *by law* such a contract is invalid, acts in ignorance *of law.* One who makes a contract with a demented person, not knowing that the person is demented, acts in ignorance *of fact.*

Ignorance is thus divided with reference to the subject *not knowing:*

Invincible ignorance, or unavoidable, is absence of knowledge under such circumstances that the knowledge *cannot* be attained.

Physically invincible ignorance is absence of knowledge under such circumstances that the knowledge cannot be attained by *any* amount of care and diligent effort.

Morally invincible ignorance is absence of knowledge under such circumstances that the knowledge cannot be attained by such an amount of care and diligence as ordinarily prudent and good men would feel obliged to put forth in the circumstances.

Vincible ignorance, or avoidable, is absence of knowledge under such circumstances that the knowledge *can* be attained, and attained *without extraordinary effort.*

4. Passion affects both intellect and will. Passions may be defined as movements of the irrational capacities of the soul, attended by a notable alteration of the body, on the apprehension of good or evil. Passions may be conveniently divided into two classes, viz., those which are movements towards the proper object of an appetite, hence a good to that appetite, and those which are reactions from something unfitting to the appetite, hence an evil to it. The first class of passions may be grouped under the general title of *concupiscence,* the second under that of *fear.* *Concupiscence* and *fear* affect both *deliberation* of the *intellect* and *freedom* of the *will.*

Non-volitional concupiscence, viz., concupiscence arising spontaneously, renders calm deliberation difficult, and, by presenting at the same time a strong attraction to the will, evidently diminishes the volitional character of the act. It sometimes renders man incapable of reason and hence entirely destroys the freedom of the act. *Volitional concupiscence,* viz., concupiscence deliberately stimulated, makes the acts consequent upon it, at least indirectly volitional, and hence imputable to the agent.

Fear is the reaction of the sensitive appetite against impending evil. When fear does not unseat reason, the actions done under its influence proceed from deliberation and free will, hence they are volitional.

5. The Particular Object of Ethics.

Oughtness or *duty* is the particular aspect under which Ethics views all volitional acts. Such acts might be viewed under their economic, political, social or artistic aspect, but Ethics considers them *solely* under the aspect of the obligation to elicit or omit them. When we say that man ought or ought not to elicit a volitional act, we imply two things: first, that the act in question is *right* and *good,* or *wrong* and *evil;* secondly, that there is an *obligation* put upon the will to elicit the good volitional act or to avoid the evil volitional act. What is this obligation, this bond, put upon the will? From the universal consent of the race, contained in the *Ethical Fact,* it is clear that the bond is not a physical bond which physically necessitates the will, for the will always remains physically free. Nor yet is this bond, according to the universal consciousness of men, a bond which arises from expediency or propriety. We are conscious that the bond placed upon us by mere social conventions is wholly different from the bond of duty which restrains us from murder. The bond put upon the will by duty is the consequence of a clear, *unconditioned dictate of reason,* commanding the will to elicit right and good volitional activity, forbidding it to elicit wrong and evil volitional activity. This peremptory and unconditioned dictate, however, leaves the will physically free to obey or disobey. Hence we say that the will is *physically free* in its volitional activity, yet *morally restricted* by oughtness or duty. And so the special object which Ethics pursues in its consideration of volitional activity is an examination and a validation of the concept of right and good, wrong and evil in human conduct, and of the concept of obligation or duty as applied to conduct.

TOPICS FOR DISCUSSION

1. Has every science a proper subject-matter and a particular view-point?
2. What are these as applied to Ethics?
3. What is the definition of a volitional act?
4. What is the meaning of deliberation?
5. Are there any voluntary acts which are not free?
6. What do you mean by a commanded act of the will?
7. Can an act of the intellect be a commanded act of the will?
8. Are commanded acts free in themselves?
9. What is an elicited act of the will?
10. What acts of man are excluded by the definition of a volitional act?
11. What are perfect and imperfect volitional acts?
12. What are directly and indirectly volitional acts?
13. What are the circumstances modifying volitional acts?

READINGS FOR CHAPTER II

Catholic Encyclopedia, "Human Acts," vol. i, p. 115; "Ignorance," vol. vii, p. 648; "Passions," vol. xi, p. 534; "Fear," vol. vi, p. 21.

Glenn, "Human Acts," chap. i, pp. 3-25.

Ross, "Human Acts," chap. ii, pp. 15-44.

Poland, "The Human Act," chap. ii, pp. 20-24, 30-41.

Leibell, "The Passions," p. 207; "Fear and Anger," p. 210; "Anger," p. 211.

Cronin, "Of Human Acts," pp. 28-45.

Keane, "Human Acts," chap. ii, pp. 25-31.

Rickaby, *Moral Philosophy,* "Of Human Acts," chap. iii, pp. 27-41; "Passions," chap. iv, pp. 41-64.

CHAPTER III

THE POSTULATES OF ETHICS

6. We have seen that the proper subject-matter of Ethics is conduct or volitional activity, likewise that the special view-point under which Ethics considers its proper subject-matter is ought-ness or duty. The first problem raised by the Ethical Fact is whether or not men are correct in judging that there is *a difference* between the right and good and the wrong and evil in human conduct.

Right in conduct has reference to *direction,* good to the *suitability* of conduct to the one who is responsible for it. Before we can say whether human conduct is right in its direction or good in its suitability to man, we must understand adequately the nature of man. If man has *no end* to be achieved by his volitional activity, then rightness or wrongness have no meaning as applied to his conduct. Similarly, without an adequate understanding of the nature of man, it is quite impossible to declare that some of his actions are *suitable* and good, others *unsuitable* and evil.

Oughtness is essentially related to *isness.* Even the virtues which an airplane should possess could not be intelligently discussed without knowing what an airplane is. If an intelligent being from Mars should visit the earth and find a watch lying in the street, such a being could perceive the hands of the watch moving, but he could not determine whether the hands were moving in the *right* direction, unless he knew the *end* for which the watch was made. Likewise such a Martian could hear the ticking of the watch, but he could not determine whether it was *suitable,* hence good, for it to tick, unless he knew the *nature* of the watch.

Hence an adequate grasp of the nature of man is absolutely essential for a true answer to the question, whether or not men judge correctly in declaring that there is a difference between right and good actions and wrong and evil actions. An examination of any entity according to the four Aristotelian causes will give a sufficiently adequate knowledge of that entity. According to Aristotle, every material entity in the visible universe is the product of at least a fourfold causality. Two of these causes, entering into the internal constitution of a being, are *intrinsic* and are called *matter* and *form.* The two others are *extrinsic* to the internal constitution of the effect and are called the *efficient* and *final* causes.

Now, the examination of man according to these four causes is made in allied branches of Philosophy, in Cosmology, in Psychology and in Natural Theodicy.

We accept the answers given there as fundamental to our science of Ethics. They are *postulates* of Ethics, but not *assumptions,* for a postulate is a truth proved in some other science.

Psychology teaches us that man is a composite being, made up of a body and soul. His body is his material cause and his soul is his formal cause. The rational soul, by its communication to the body, is the vital principle of man's vegetative and sensitive life as well as of his rational life. It is the formal principle which determines man to exist as a unitary whole in that particular species of being which we call a rational animal. Man has many activities of the vegetative and sensitive life, but all these are for his rational life, and the subordination of these to the rational tendency and supreme appetite in man makes man a unitary whole. If man had as many supreme tendencies as he has faculties, he would not be a unitary whole. To be a unitary whole, an entity must have one paramount and supreme tendency, in virtue of which it tends to the end of that nature as a complete whole. The *supreme tendency* or *appetite* in man is the *rational will:* it is a tendency toward the *good* of man as a *unitary whole.* Since the will is the supreme expression of man's tendency as a unitary whole, it will be possible to determine the *ultimate end* of man himself, if we can determine what is that *ultimate good* for which the will has a capacity and towards which it has an impulse. This we do in the second thesis. Thus we say that man is a being composed of body and soul, and that the body is *for* and *subordinated to* the tendencies of the rational soul expressed through its supreme appetite, the will.

If we are to seek the absolutely ultimate efficient and final causes of man as well as of all other things in the visible universe, we must turn to the sound conclusions of Cosmology and Theodicy. There we learn that the ultimate efficient cause of all things is the First Cause, God, Who is an intelligent, personal, infinitely perfect Being. God brought all things into existence by a unique kind of efficient causality, which is called creation, i.e., the production of an entity without any antecedent subject-matter from which it is produced.

Since God is infinitely perfect, i.e., since He contains in Himself, in some way, all possible perfections, the products of His creative activity must be imitations of His own perfections. All created natures, therefore, are imitations of Divine perfections and can perform, in virtue of their created perfection, some activity which God can do in virtue of His uncreated perfection.

7. Two profound and far-reaching truths flow from this. First, since each created nature has a capacity to do, in virtue of

that nature, some specific activity, which is an imitation of some
Divine activity, it is the will of the Author of that nature that it
perform just that specific activity,—for by that activity it expresses
some Divine activity and some Divine perfection.   Hence all
created natures, by the performance of their specific activities,
manifest Divine perfections.   Now, the manifestation of excellence
is *fundamental* glory; wherefore all natures, by their manifestation
of God's perfections, are His fundamental glory.   Thus we have
learned that the manifestation of Divine perfection, or the fundamental glory of God, is the final cause of all created entities.   Man,
being the most perfect being in the visible universe, must share in
the Divine perfection in a higher way.   He must be able to do
something in virtue of his created nature which God does in virtue
of His uncreated nature, something at the same time which distinguishes him from all other created natures in the visible universe.   In other words, he must be able to do something in virtue
of the *specific* nature which distinguishes him from all other created entities.   The distinguishing characteristics of man's nature
are *intellect* and *will*.   Hence man will do, in virtue of his created
intellect and will, what God does in virtue of those perfections of
His of which man's intellect and will are imitations.

Now, the proper objects of man's intellect and will, as demonstrated in Psychology, are *universal truth* and *universal good*.
Hence man is destined by his specific nature to the possession of
universal truth by his intellect and the possession of universal good
by his will.   But as God alone is universal truth and universal
good, possessing as He does in Himself all perfections, man is
destined by his specific nature to *know* and *love God*.   This knowledge and love of God is God's *formal* glory, for formal glory is
the acknowledgment and praise of excellence.   Therefore, the *final
purpose* of man in the universe, as judged by his specific nature,
is God's formal glory, i.e., the knowledge and love of universal
truth and good, just as the final purpose of all other created entities in the universe is God's *fundamental* glory, i.e., the manifestation of Divine excellence.   Man rises to the knowledge and love of
God by a consideration of His perfections manifested in the universe.   Without intelligent creatures such as man, the universe
would be a book without a reader or an organ with no one to touch
its keys.   Since man is a microcosm altogether dependent upon the
visible universe, since he draws from it means of sustenance, conservation and development, since he is its highest expression, its
lord and master—the universe, through man as its spokesman,
knowing and loving God's infinite perfection, gives formal glory
to God.   *This is the Divine plan in creation.*

The second profound truth which flows from what we have seen is this: God, being infinitely wise and holy, i.e., wedded to order, cannot be indifferent to the fulfilment of His plan. He must *will* that all creatures play their proper parts in the harmonious plan of creation. His will is so impressed upon all other creatures, except man in his free nature, that they are *physically* compelled to fulfil their parts. This will of God impressed upon all creatures except man *in his free nature* is physical law, in virtue of which every non-free nature, under the conditions proper for its exercise, must, by physical necessity, perform its connatural activity. This physical law is also stamped upon the lower nature of man, and it completely governs all those actions of his which are not subject to volitional activity. Only the *will* of man, and the *lower faculties subject to its control,* are not always physically necessitated. Nevertheless this does not mean that man, physically free in his will, is not subject to the *will* of God commanding him to play his part in the harmony of nature and to give God formal glory by knowledge and love of Divine excellence. How man's will, though *physically* free, is *morally* bound is the subject of another chapter. It is only necessary to remember this: God as infinitely wise and holy cannot be *indifferent* as to whether or not man achieves that for which his specific nature has a capacity and towards which it has an impulse, the knowledge and love of God.

We have thus considered the *isness* of man according to the four Aristotelian causes. He is a unitary whole composed of body and soul. His ultimate efficient cause is God and his ultimate final cause is God's formal *extrinsic* glory. *God's formal intrinsic* glory is the result of the knowledge and love God has of His own infinite perfections. These truths are postulates of Ethics.

TOPICS FOR DISCUSSION

1. What is the general meaning of the terms, *right* and *good?*
2. What is a necessary implication of the terms, *right* and *good,* when applied to volitional activity?
3. Why is it necessary in Ethics to have an adequate understanding of the nature of man?
4. How can we gain this adequate knowledge?
5. Do we demonstrate in Ethics the knowledge we have of man according to the four Aristotelian causes?
6. Is this knowledge an assumption?
7. What are the two intrinsic causes of man?
8. What do you mean when you say that man is a unitary whole?
9. What faculties show the specific nature of man?
10. What faculty exhibits the supreme tendency in man?
11. Why do we call the will an appetite? Why a rational appetite?
12. What is the absolutely ultimate efficient cause of man and the universe?

13. By what distinctive type of efficient causality did God bring the universe into being?
14. What is the nature of the First Cause?
15. Are all created natures imitations of Divine perfections? Why?
16. Can all created natures perform, in virtue of their natures, some actions which God can perform in virtue of His uncreated nature?
17. Is it the necessary will of God that under proper conditions created natures perform these actions?
18. Do they manifest God's perfections by their specific activity?
19. What is glory? Intrinsic glory? Fundamental glory? Formal glory?
20. Do all creatures manifest God's glory? His intrinsic or His extrinsic glory? His fundamental or His formal glory?
21. Must man manifest God's perfections in a distinctive way? Why?
22. Is it God's purpose in creating the universe that man glorify Him by knowledge and love?
23. Does the whole universe, as summed up in man, give formal glory to God?
24. Since all other creatures are subordinated to man, i.e., are for his good, would you say that the extrinsic end of these creatures is man, just as the extrinsic end of man is God's formal glory?
25. Does what we have considered constitute a Divine plan of the universe?
26. Must God will effectively that His plan be carried out?
27. Is God's will implanted effectively in the natures of irrational creatures?
28. Does God's will in this respect produce physical necessity?
29. Does God's will produce physical necessity in man?

READINGS FOR CHAPTER III

Leibell, The Postulates, chap. ii, pp. 35-155.
Sullivan, *Limitations of Science,* chap. vi, pp. 197-239.
Drawbridge, the whole book.
Hull, the whole book. - *Why should I be moral?*

CHAPTER IV

THE END OF HUMAN ACTION

THESIS I

The natural and proper end of man is known from his nature, or from all his faculties subordinated to one specific tendency. This tendency, or proper final activity of human nature, is manifested by the will. In the individual acts of the will, man, interpretatively at least, intends his absolutely ultimate end.

Explanation of the Thesis

8. The natural *termination* of an action, *good,* and *end, objectively* and *materially* signify the same thing. The reason why a faculty is solicited to a motion of tendency towards some object is because that object is capable of conferring a suitable perfection. Whatever is suitable to the perfection of a nature is *good.* The same *term* of an *action,* which is called a good, inasfar as it regards the perfection of a nature or of its faculties, is called *end,* in a *general* sense, since by it the natural tendency is *ended.* In a more *specific* sense, *end,* together with the idea of *term,* also implies the idea of causality, in so far as the *term* apprehended by the intellect as a *good* has a bearing on the constitution of an appetite.

9. The end is *proximate, mediate* or *ultimate,* in so far as it is *immediately* attained by the agent, or is attained by the agent only to be *referred* to some further end, or is the *last thing* which is attained. Suarez explains how an end, viz., something which is desired because of itself, and on account of which other things are desired, may be called *proximate* or *mediate.* Two elements belong to an end in its proper sense. The first is, that it should be loved *on account of itself,* in which notion is included the denial of relationship of this *end* to another; and hence it is that every *end* looked at precisely under the formality of *end* has the characteristic of something *ultimate.* It happens, however, that some particular good may be loved because of its intrinsic goodness and at the same time may be referred to some ulterior end. For this reason we must not confuse a mere *useful good* with a *proximate* or a *mediate end:* for a useful good is only called good through extrinsic denomination.

Such a *proximate* or *mediate* end is called non-ultimate, because, although under one respect it participates in the causality of *end,* nevertheless the will does not rest in it, but proceeds further. That *end* is called *absolutely ultimate* in which the will rests without referring it to anything else. It is ultimate in execution, because once it is attained the motor-tendency of the will ceases. The second characteristic of an end in the proper sense is that other things are loved *on account of it*. For this reason the division already made can be explained in another way. There is a certain end which is called simply or *absolutely ultimate*. When such an end is attained, the nature of the agent is such that by this attainment the nature is *perfectly completed*, and there is nothing else remaining towards which the agent may extend itself. There is another ultimate end only *under a certain aspect*, or *ultimate* in some series, as, for instance, health is said to be the ultimate end of medicine because everything which belongs to the art of medicine is referred to this end and proceeds no further. The first end is called *absolutely, simply* and *positively ultimate;* the second end is called *relatively ultimate*.

10. An end is called *end of the work* or *end of the agent*, according as it is that towards which the *entity*, the *work* or *action* tends by its nature, or according as it is that which the *agent* wishes to achieve by means of the activity.

11. An end is *intrinsic* and *extrinsic*, according as it is that to which the agent is directed by its nature and that which constitutes the internal perfection of the agent, or according as it is that to which by the design and ordination of the one constituting the nature, the nature is referred. Hence the end of man can be considered in a twofold way, viz., from the aspect of man, the creature, and from the aspect of God, the Creator. The latter end is called *primary* and is the *external glory of God;* the first is called *secondary* and is the *ultimate perfection of the rational creature*. These two ends are the same in actuality, but distinct by reason. The second is treated in Cosmology and Natural Theology; the first in Ethics.

12. An end is an *end which,* an *end for whom* and an *end by which*. An *end which* is said to be the *good* for the attainment of which the will operates, as, e.g., health. The *end for whom* is said to be the *person* or the *subject* for whom some good is loved or sought, as, e.g., the man who seeks health for himself is the *end for whom* of health. The *end by which* is the *attainment* of the good sought. The *end which* and the *end by which* are related to each other as a thing *attained* and the *attainment* of the thing, and are sometimes called the *objective end* and the *formal end,* which are not two distinct ends, but integrate one end. The reason for this is that the object cannot be attained except through an act, nor can the act exist except in relation to an object; and thus the intention and motions of the agent for achieving an act and an object are one and the same thing.

If the *end which* and the *end for whom* are compared to each other, there arises a difficulty as to which of these is the principal end. For if the good for the sake of which a man operates is apprehended as something as noble as himself or more noble than himself, then that good cannot be correctly ordered to himself, as an end. Hence when a man loves this good for himself, he does not order it to himself *as an end,* but rather desires to be joined to that good *as a good.* Much more true is this if the *end which* is the *supreme good* in respect to the one for whom it is desired. Hence it follows that the *end which* and the *end for whom,* compared to one another, are not vested with the characteristic of end. Although, e.g., man loves God as a good for man himself, nevertheless, he does not order God to himself as to an end, but he himself is ordered to God as the last end; not, however, as a means properly so-called, but as a subject which can attain this end.

13. The will tends towards an end in four ways:

(A) *Actually,* if the will here and now, moved by the end, elicits or commands an act.

(B) *Virtually,* if the operation proceeds from an act of the will formerly elicited, which is not recalled, but remains in some effect of the preceding action and thus remains "in power" or virtually.

(C) *Habitually,* if an activity exists from a previous actual motion of the will related to an end, and although the previous intention was not recalled, the action goes on without the actual influence of the first intention.

(D) *Interpretatively,* if the agent in none of the previous ways intends an end, but the action, by its very nature, tends to an end and the agent does not positively exclude it. Thus we *interpret* that the agent would intend the end towards which the activity tends by its nature, if the end is not *positively* excluded.

14. It is disputed how it can be that all human actions are on account of some ultimate end. The Thomists in general and others hold that all human actions are on account of some ultimate end, habitually intended, which end is at least relatively ultimate. Another question is, whether all human actions are on account of the absolutely ultimate end, considered not objectively but subjectively, i.e., on account of a perfect and complete good of man, although it is not necessary that the subject in which that characteristic of good is contained should be apprehended by reason. Scotus, whose opinion Suarez holds, declares that it is not absolutely necessary that, antecedent to the intention and the ten-

dency towards particular good, the intention of the last end looked at objectively or subjectively should precede. It is sufficient, according to Scotus, that the will should be moved by some good object of its nature lovable, which includes in itself the common characteristic of good and virtually contains in some way, at least implicitly and interpretatively, the last end. The thesis has three parts.

FIRST PART

The natural and proper end of man is known from his nature, or from all his faculties subordinated to one specific tendency.

Proof

15. The natural and proper end of man is that good of man, perfective of man as a *specific* entity, toward which man tends by a natural appetite.

But the good of man, perfective of man as a *specific* entity, towards which man tends by a natural appetite, is known from his nature or from all his faculties subordinated to one specific tendency.

Therefore, the natural and proper end of man is known from his nature or from all his faculties subordinated to one specific tendency.

Proof of the Major:

This follows from the correlation between the object of an appetite or the end of its activity and the appetite itself.

Proof of the Minor:

The Minor follows from the fact that faculties, as proceeding from nature, manifest the natural tendency of that nature; the *specific* tendency, if they tend towards the good of the *whole* nature; the *generic* tendency, if they tend towards the good of one or another faculty.

SECOND PART

This tendency or proper final activity of human nature is manifested by the will.

Proof

16. The natural tendency of man as a specific entity is that which directs all his particular tendencies to unity, similar to a resultant unity in some system of mechanical forces.

But the will manifests such a directive tendency.

Therefore, the will manifests the natural tendency of man as a specific entity or the proper final activity of human nature.

Proof of the Major:

Every composite, which is *per se one,* constitutes a nature or principle of operation *per se one;* and hence the natural and proper tendency of the whole nature or composite is *one.* But man is a composite entity *per se one.* Therefore, the natural tendency of man as a specific entity directs all the particular tendencies to unity.

Proof of the Minor:

Man, as a natural composite, arising from body and soul, and as a constant nature, has a twofold class of tendencies: one, which corresponds to his rational nature and consists in his *rational appetite* or *will;* the other, which is found in his animal nature and consists in his *sensitive appetite.* The vegetative and inorganic tendencies of man, since they are assumed by physical necessity for the service of animal life and are immediately subordinated to this by the unity of his nature, can be classed in the tendencies of man's *animal* nature. But for these different tendencies to be directed to the unity of a composite nature, it is necessary that all should be subservient and subordinate to one tendency which is supreme and therefore to the rational tendency or the will. Therefore, the will manifests in man the natural tendency of man as such.

THIRD PART

In the individual acts of the will man interpretatively at least intends his absolutely ultimate end.

Proof

17. Man in his individual acts intends some particular good. Hence (1) he intends some good which either partially or inchoatively is referred to his complete and perfect good; (2) he does not positively exclude the ordination of this particular good to his perfect good subjectively looked at.

But for man to tend towards a good which by its very nature is referred to a perfect good and not positively to exclude such a reference to a perfect good, is to intend his absolutely ultimate end at least *interpretatively.*

Therefore, in his individual acts at least *interpretatively* man intends his absolutely ultimate end.

Proof of the Major:

(1) A particular good is a good, in so far as it is a participation and an inchoation of perfect good. Therefore, from its very

nature it is referred to a perfect good. (2) The object of the will is *good,* and so, although the will may reject a good looked at objectively, viz., a thing in which a characteristic of good is found, it is unable positively to exclude whatever is a good in its subjective sense, viz., the characteristic of perfect good.

Proof of the Minor:

The Minor is evident from the definition of interpretative intention.

TOPICS FOR DISCUSSION

1. Is there any difference between the *natural termination* of *an action, good,* and *end?*
2. Can a mere means to an end be designated as a good in the proper sense?
3. Are the *end which* and the *end by which* two perfectly distinct ends?
4. Is the *end which* always subordinated to the *end for which?*
5. Does moderate eating without any thought of its purpose *interpretatively* tend towards the last end of the will?
6. Why does the will manifest the final tendency of human nature?
7. Is the will an appetite? A rational appetite?

THESIS II

The absolutely ultimate intrinsic end of man's volitional activity is perfect happiness or beatitude, really to be attained.

Explanation of the Thesis

18. From the consideration of the third chapter we have a fairly adequate, though not completely comprehensive, idea of man. We stated there that it would be possible to determine the ultimate end of man himself by an analysis of the *capacity* and *tendency* of his will. We proceed in this chapter to determine precisely the ultimate end of man from an analysis of his will.

An *end* is that for the sake of which something is done. For example, indication of time is the end of a watch, the purpose for which it is made. It may also be made for the purpose of gain. This latter is likewise an end. An *end,* therefore, may be either an *end of the work* or an *end of the agent* or both.

An end of work is that end towards which an entity tends of its very nature, i.e., that for the production or acquisition of which a being is *in itself proportioned* and towards which in consequence it has a *native tendency.* To illustrate: flying is the *end of work* of an airplane. The question with which we are concerned is the *end of work* of the *will.*

An end of agent is that end which a rational agent intends to effect or acquire by his activity. The end of the agent, the purpose of God in creating the will, is His own extrinsic glory.

An end of work is either *extrinsic* or *intrinsic.* It is *intrinsic,* when the end is realizable within the nature of the being in question through a perfection of which the being is capable. It is *extrinsic,* when the end is realizable outside of the nature of the being in question, to which end the intrinsic perfection of the being has been directed by its author.

Ends are also divided into *proximate, intermediate,* and *ultimate relatively* or *absolutely,* as explained in the first thesis.

In this thesis, we are considering the *end of work,* i.e., we are asking and answering the question, "What is the end for the production or acquisition of which the will is *proportioned* and for which consequently it has a *natural tendency?"* Secondly, we are inquiring about the *intrinsic end* of the will, viz., about that end which is to be realized within the will itself. Thirdly, we are asking about the *absolutely ultimate intrinsic end,* the one, in other words, which will completely exhaust the capacity of the will for desiring. As is obvious, we are not concerned with those *particular* ends which the will sets before itself in its various activities, but about that end which is set before it by the Author of Nature, the end for which it has a *capacity* and towards which it has an *impulse.*

19. *Perfect happiness* or *beatitude* is the full and enduring possession of *supreme* and *perfect good.* The supreme and perfect good for rational nature is the *ultimate perfection* of that nature and the *enjoyment* consequent upon it. It implies the possession of a good giving full satisfaction to the rational appetite. The concept of beatitude contains three elements: the first is *negative,* the exclusion of all evil; the second is *positive,* the full possession of all good connaturally possible; the third is *complementary,* perpetual permanence known with certitude. Beatitude can be divided into *essential* and *accidental beatitude.* Many *goods* are found in the beatified; but it is not by all of these that he attains his last end. Beatitude implies the ultimate perfection to which all other *goods* are referred. *Essential* beatitude does not consist in the total collection of *goods,* but in that good which is supreme and ultimate. In this and the two subsequent theses, there is question of *essential* beatitude.

20. Beatitude can be considered in a threefold way. First, with regard to the object in the possession of which man is beatified. This is *objective* beatitude. Secondly, with regard to the act by which the subject beatified possesses the beatifying object, viz., the act by which man's specific faculties rest in the possession of the supreme good.   This is *formal* beatitude.   Thirdly, with regard to the permanent state in which the possession of the beatifying object is enjoyed without limit.   This is *subjective* beatitude, and of this there is question in the present thesis.   In other words, we consider here *beatitude indeterminately* as a subjective state, abstracting from the object in the possession of which it consists and from the particular mode or manner whereby the object is possessed.

Proof of the Thesis

21.   The absolutely ultimate intrinsic end of man's volitional activity consists in that to which the will, in virtue of its *innate* appetite and also of its *elicited* appetite, is *ultimately* drawn by nature.

But in virtue of both these appetites the will is *ultimately* drawn by nature to beatitude, really to be attained.

Therefore, the absolutely ultimate intrinsic end of man's volitional activity is beatitude, really to be attained.

Explanation

22.   To understand the argument it must be noted that appetite is twofold, *innate* and *elicited*.   An *elicited* appetite is a tendency towards a good known by reason or by sense.   An *innate* appetite is an inclination towards an object by an interior principle *without cognition*.   This latter is a quasi-gravitation of nature impressed upon a being by the Author of Nature.   It implies a *capacity* for that towards which it is inclined and a *positive tendency* by which the appetite is urged towards its good.   It is asserted that this twofold appetite of the will indicates the *absolutely ultimate intrinsic end* of volitional activity.

Proof of the Major:

With regard to the *innate* appetite of the will: an innate tendency, which cannot be positively rejected and which at the same time implies a *capacity* for that towards which the appetite is ultimately directed, indicates the *ultimate natural end* of that appetite, the end intended by nature and by the will of the Creator.

With regard to the *elicited* appetite of the will: the elicited appetite by actual appetition either explicitly or implicitly tends to that towards which it is in general directed by the innate appetite. For the elicited appetite of the will is a tendency towards an object apprehended by reason as good, and though the intellect may err in proposing to it an object only apparently good, nevertheless the elicited appetite is nothing else than a cognoscitive actuation of an essential and natural innate appetite.

Proof of the Minor:

With regard to the *innate* appetite of the will: the will is drawn in virtue of this appetite to universal good, viz., to all good looked at *indeterminately,* as is proved in Psychology. But this formal object of the will is the same as subjective beatitude.

With regard to the *elicited* appetite of the will: experience testifies that the elicited appetite of the will is never fully satiated, but always aims invincibly at further good. But it is repugnant to the Divine perfections of the Creator that this invincible inclination of the will should not be aimed at an *existent* good which will satiate it, viz., at beatitude, really to be attained. Therefore, in virtue of its elicited appetite, the will is by nature drawn to beatitude, really to be attained.

N.B.—It is contrary to the *Divine wisdom* to insert in rational nature an invincible tendency to a motion for which there is no real term. It is against the *Divine fidelity* to attract man by a kind of promise impressed upon his nature for which there is no fulfilment. It is opposed to the *Divine goodness* to saddle man with an insatiable appetite of which he is conscious and which could never be satisfied.

Corollaries

23. Not only the end of the will, but also the *end of man* is beatitude, really to be attained, since the will is his *supreme* and *specific* appetite.

24. In the argument there is question only of the tendency of the will which is *formally* natural, i.e., of that tendency which constitutes the essence of the will and is, therefore, plainly necessary and invincible. This formal tendency is *exclusively* the desire of complete happiness or of the possession of universal good. Whatever man seeks in particular, under the impulse of this desire, is desired not through a necessity of nature, but rather *according* to nature through the election of the will. Therefore, it is not necessary that every such desire be fulfilled.

25. There is no parity in this matter between man and the brute animal. In the first place, the total nature of the brute, with all its potencies and appetites, is subjected to man by the Author of Nature. Secondly, since animals are incapable of forming a universal concept, they can never actually desire anything except a sensible object, and hence they have no tendency towards beatitude. Thirdly, the attainment of the intrinsic end of animals is *conditioned* upon the utility and service of man, for which they are made. Man, on the other hand, is *directly* ordered to God, as

will be proved in the next thesis and, therefore, the attainment of his intrinsic perfection is not conditioned upon the utility and service of any other created being.

Scholia

26. The opinion of Kant, placing the natural end of man in a perpetual approach to beatitude never to be really attained, is excluded by our argument.

27. Similar to Kant's view are the opinions of those ethicians who place the end of man or (as they say) of humanity in a constant evolution and progress towards an ideal culture and perfection.

TOPICS FOR DISCUSSION

1. With what end of the will are we concerned in this thesis?
2. What are the three elements contained in the concept of beatitude?
3. What are the three ways in which beatitude may be considered? In what respect do we consider beatitude in this thesis?
4. What are the two kinds of appetite which we consider in establishing the truth of our thesis?
5. How is it contrary to the perfections of God to lure man on by a desire for beatitude never to be fulfilled?
6. Why is the end of man's will also the end of man?
7. Why cannot we argue to the non-attainment of man's final end from the fact that animals often fail to attain their intrinsic end?

THESIS III

The object sufficient of its nature and necessary for man's beatitude is God alone.

Explanation of the Thesis

28. There is question in this thesis of *objective* beatitude, viz., of that object, the attainment of which confers upon man perfect happiness or the ultimate perfection of his rational nature. That such an object exists is a corollary of the second thesis, wherein it was proved that it is quite out of conformity with the Divine perfections to give man a formally natural tendency towards something which does not exist. What that object is we disclose in this thesis, viz.: the First Cause, Who is a necessary and infinitely perfect Being. The question in this thesis is on essential beatitude as explained in No. 19.

Proof of the Thesis

29. The object sufficient of its nature and necessary for man's essential beatitude must have the capacity to satiate man's natural specific tendencies in such wise that: (1) all evil is altogether excluded; (2) all good of which the beatified is capable is possessed; (3) this possession is perpetual.

But God alone is such an object.

Therefore, the object sufficient of its nature and necessary for man's beatitude is God alone.

Proof of the Major:

It is presupposed, in view of the truth of the second thesis, that there is an object of beatitude. Moreover, it is evident that, in virtue of such an object: (1) all evil must be altogether excluded by the nature of beatitude in so far as it is a correlative of the innate tendency of the will; (2) all good of which the beatified is capable must be perfectly possessed for the same reason; (3) again as a consequence of the nature of beatitude, the possession of this object must be perpetual. If the possession were not perpetual, all evil would not be excluded, nor would every good of which the beatified is capable be possessed. The blessed would either know that they could lose the state of beatitude or that it might come to an end, or they would be ignorant of these two possibilities. On the first supposition they would be unhappy; on the second they would be in error because of the nature of the innate appetite of the will, which persuades us that the state of beatitude is perpetual, or at least they would be in a state of doubt and terror lest they lose this state. Such an error would be a great evil in itself and attributable to the Author of Nature, and the uncertainty and fear would be contrary to the state of beatitude.

Proof of the Minor:

The Minor is an exclusive proposition and consequently must be proved both negatively and positively.

A. **Negative Proof:** All created goods can be reduced to three heads: (1) External goods or goods of fortune, which do not affect man intrinsically; (2) goods intrinsically affecting man in his body; (3) goods intrinsically affecting man in his soul, by which we mean either the soul itself, or perfections inhering in the soul, or spiritual goods acquired through the exercise of its faculties. But the object of beatitude can be found neither in any one of these nor in any assemblage of these. Therefore, the object of beatitude cannot be found in created goods.

The proof of the second minor proceeds as follows: (1) Goods of fortune are of an inferior order and cannot satisfy an appetite of a superior order such as the will. They are extrinsic and instrumental and cannot perfect man in himself. They are perishable, uncertain and unstable. (2) Goods of the body are inferior to those of the soul and are common to both men and animals. But man is capable of beatitude, not according to that which he has in common with animals, but according to that by which he is man. Moreover, like goods of fortune, they are instrumental, uncertain and unstable. (3) The created goods of the soul are, in the first place, the soul itself, which is the subject of beatitude, but cannot be its object, inasmuch as it cannot be the end of itself and hence find quiescence in itself. So much is evident from the fact that it always possesses itself, yet is not happy in itself, but always seeks something extrinsic to itself. Goods of the soul, in the second place, are its potencies and acts, which are less perfect goods than the soul itself and for the same reasons as those given above cannot be the object of beatitude. Goods of the soul, in the third place, are the spiritual goods acquired by the exercise of its faculties. These are rather a disposition for acquiring beatitude than beatitude itself; for wisdom is nothing else than the knowledge of true good and the desire to acquire it, and virtue a habit fostered by this knowledge and by free activity in accordance with it, and neither wisdom nor virtue perfectly satisfy the innate appetite of the will for perfect good. (4) All created goods together are insufficient for conferring beatitude upon man: first, because individual created goods are insufficient to attain this end, not by reason of quantity, but by reason of quality; secondly, because uncreated truth and uncreated good are evidently to be included in the formal objects of the intellect and the will; and lastly, because an assemblage of these created goods, e.g., voluptuousness and virtue, would necessarily involve repugnance.

B. **Positive Proof:** That *alone* can perfectly satisfy man's natural and specific tendencies in the manner explained in the major, which in reality is commensurate with the formal objects of the intellect and will. For a perfect good, which will quiet man's natural and specific tendencies, in which satiation man's essential beatitude consists, ought to be loved because of itself, and never because of something else. No good can achieve this unless it is in reality commensurate with the formal objects of the intellect and the will. The formal objects of each of these faculties are universal in extent, viz., in the order of *cognition,* whatever is *true,* and in the order of *volition,* whatever is *good.* Moreover, God *alone* is an object which corresponds to and is commensurate with the universal-in-tendency of the faculties of intellect and will. For God *alone* is unlimited truth and unlimited good. Hence God *alone* is the object which in reality is commensurate with the formal objects of the intellect and will.

TOPICS FOR DISCUSSION

1. With what kind of beatitude is the present thesis concerned? Explain your answer.
2. Why must the object of beatitude exclude all evil? Supply all good to the subject beatified? Be perpetually possessed?
3. In what three classes can created goods be grouped?
4. Why cannot goods of fortune be the object of beatitude? Goods of the body? Goods of the soul?
5. Is the predicate of inability to satisfy man's rational appetite an essential predicate of all created goods? Is this the primary reason why no assemblage of such goods can be the object of beatitude?
6. With the objects of what appetites must the object of beatitude be in reality commensurate?
7. Explain your method of arriving at the fact that God alone is so commensurate.

THESIS IV

Beatitude formally consists in the perfect knowledge and perfect love of God.

Explanation of the Thesis

30. We have now considered beatitude *subjectively* and *objectively*. It remains to consider beatitude *formally,* viz., according to the form by which the beatified is united with the beatifying object. Beatitude *formally considered* signifies a certain perfection with which the beatified is *informed,* or a most *perfect operation* by which the beatifying object is possessed. Since beatitude is the ultimate perfection of man, it must consist in some operation, inasmuch as every entity is perfect to the extent that it is in operation, and inasmuch as a potency without activity is imperfect.

31. The question arises whether beatitude consists in one or in many operations. From the very nature of the case, many operations are required for beatitude *adequately* considered, and without them no one could be considered truly blessed. They are: *knowledge,* without which there can be neither joy nor love; *love,* which is necessary that knowledge may lead to the possession of the supreme good; *joy,* which is necessarily consequent upon the knowledge and love of the supreme good. Philosophically, these are correlative acts and mutually complete the proper activity of the whole nature, and they are therefore necessary for the satiation of the whole nature. Finally, it is evident that, though many operations are required for the *integrity* of the beatific state, only those actions by which the beatifying object is formally and immediately possessed can pertain to the *essence* of that state. Conse-

quently, (1) the operation of the senses, on the supposition that for perfect beatitude in the state of nature, union of the soul with the body is necessarily required, does not enter into the essence of beatitude; (2) the operations of the intellect and will which have not God for their immediate object do not pertain to the essence of the beatific state.

32. Passing over the many controversies which have arisen with regard to this matter, we maintain that the *physical essence* of beatitude *formally considered* consists in the perfect knowledge and perfect love of God, of which two operations joy is the necessary consequence.

Proof of the Thesis

33. Beatitude formally consists in the perfect operation of those faculties which are apt and destined for union with God.

But only the intellect and will are apt and destined for union with God.

Therefore, beatitude formally consists in the perfect operation of these two faculties, viz., in perfect knowledge and perfect love of God.

Proof of the Major:

We have already proved that man is destined for beatitude and that the only object capable of conferring this beatitude is God. Therefore, beatitude will formally consist in the operation of those faculties by which God is possessed and indeed in their *perfect* operation. For if the capacity of these faculties to possess God be not exhausted, they will tend towards further possession, and until this tendency is satisfied, beatitude will be impossible.

Proof of the Minor:

Only the intellect and will are apt and destined for the possession of God, for only these faculties are objectively infinite, i.e., tend in virtue of their formal objects to that which is unlimited.

Scholia

34. That God may be the object of human beatitude, there is no necessity for an *entitative* proportion between human nature and the Divine nature. A proportion of *final* relationship is sufficient.

35. The indivisibility of God does not exclude different degrees of beatitude in different subjects. This difference does not arise from the object, which is always possessed as a whole, but from natural capacity, which cannot be infinite in a created being and

hence can vary in degree according to the varying capacity of the one beatified.

36. God is not a means which man uses for self-beatification, but is the object causing beatitude, i.e., He is the absolute center of all final order, to Whom man himself, beatified in God, is ultimately subjected. Cf. p. 15, supra, No. 12.

37. It follows from this thesis that man is directly and immediately ordered to God. Hence, as we have already indicated, man is not subordinated to any other order of being. The case of irrational creatures is exactly the contrary. They are directly ordered to the utility of man, who is their immediate end. The attainment of the intrinsic end of animals is conditioned by their subservience to man. Hence when man destroys an animal he does not violate the order of its being. On the other hand, the immediate ordering of every individual man to God by his specific faculties of intellect and will is the basis of that inviolate individual independence and dignity from which human rights have their origin.

38. The beatitude which we have been considering is *natural* beatitude, the natural end of man, arrived at by considering the natural end of man's faculties and by abstracting from the *supernatural* end of man consequent upon his elevation to a supernatural state of Divine grace. God is the object whose possession beatifies man whether we consider his beatitude from the natural or the supernatural standpoint. However, in supernatural beatitude, God is possessed by intuitive, face-to-face knowledge, i.e., He is known as He is in Himself and not merely through His effects. Such knowledge is called the beatific vision. The philosopher does not consider beatitude from this view-point.

39. Although beatitude, proximately considered, has reference to the good of man, by the desire of which he loves himself, nevertheless beatitude neither uniquely nor principally embraces the good of man as such. It principally embraces the glorification of God, which is necessarily contained in the beatitude of man and to which the beatitude of man is subordinated. For man cannot attain beatitude, i.e., the perfect knowledge and love of God, without concomitantly compassing God's glory. The perfect knowledge and love of God, in which man's beatitude consists, necessarily involve the extrinsic formal glory of God, to which man's subjective intrinsic perfection is necessarily referred as to its extrinsic end. Thus by a marvelous manifestation of Divine wisdom, just as objectively by one and the same act man is beatified and God is glorified, so subjectively when the human will tends towards its true beatitude, it is in agreement with the necessary order of things.

40. Man's beatitude consists in the exercise of his intellect and will upon their infinite object and in the enjoyment consequent upon such exercise. This enjoyment is the complete satisfaction of man's *specifically* vital faculties. Hence beatitude is not a cessation from activity, but rather a cessation from striving after further objects, since all such objects are contained in the infinite object now possessed through perfect knowledge and love.

Erroneous Opinions with Regard to the Ultimate End of Man

41. Many moderns either say that we are ignorant of the end of man, or, rejecting a "transcendental," "metaphysical" and "absolute" end, acknowledge only a terrestrial good of man. This terrestrial good is, according to some, an *individual* good, viz., the perfection of one's own personality, or a *social* good, viz., the prosperity and cultural development of the human race, or both together. We pass over here the older philosophers who held these views, because later on we explain them in treating of the norm of morality.

The *good of the individual* is now often declared to be the end of man. It is said that the *supreme destiny* of life consists in "The development of free personality." In general this doctrine conceives the individual after the manner of an *absolute being,* as emancipated from God and a future life, as altogether independent and merely transitory. Human nature in this opinion is held to be altogether good and to be cultivated as a whole. Its viciousness is ignored. Modern pantheism, which declares man to be the noblest manifestation of the absolute, fits in with these conceptions. These ideas have taken many forms. Sometimes the perfection of man is too much restricted, as when the cultivation of the intellect alone, or of the body alone or solely of the æsthetic sense is advocated. Sometimes the opinion is held that the cultivation of the individual is to be sought by indulgence of all the inclinations of nature with neglect of all moral law or social good. Sometimes there is asserted "the right to sin," since man has the power to follow the law of his nature, viz., sensuality, and since by sin man manifests his strength and liberty. Nietzsche advocated this extreme form of individualism and not a few of those who hold religious morality in contempt venerate him as a prophet.

Let us take a few illustrations from those who advocate this cult of personality. F. Paulsen declares: "The highest good of man . . . is a life, in which personality is fully and harmoniously developed and all its powers are exercised." J. M. Guyau says: *"Ce principe, nous croyons y'avoir trouvé dans la vie la plus intensive et la plus extensive possible, sous la rapporte physique et mental."* F. Thilly says: "We have found thus far, I believe, that the preservation and promotion of individual and social life is the highest good, or the end aimed at by humanity, in the sense explained before." G. Mehlis teaches: "The principle of individualism holds that we are obliged to form personality solely by our own individuality." Kant prepared the way for this philosophy by his doctrine that rational nature is an end in itself, and is therefore autonomous, bound solely by its own law.

Nietzsche (died 1900) developed this cult of personality into his perverted egoism. He taught that man must gradually be developed into a higher species, viz., the superman. Hence all those who feel themselves stronger than others and experience in themselves the power of ascending higher have the right freely to develop their powers without restriction from any superior law. Everything is lawful to those who have the will to power, even the suppression of the weak. This *morality* he proposed for the lords of the world; to others he left the *morality of slaves,* in his opinion, *Christian morality,* which teaches mercy, humility and obedience.

From contemporary writings we select the following: "When I shall die I shall be content to vanish into nothingness. No show, however good, could conceivably be good forever." (H. L. Mencken.) "If I go to a play I do not enjoy it less because I do not believe it is Divinely created and Divinely conducted, that it will last forever instead of stopping at eleven, that many details of it will remain in my memory, or that it will have any particular moral effect upon me. And I enjoy life as I enjoy that play." (Sinclair Lewis.) Both of these take mechanism or materialism for granted. "The collapse of organized supernatural religion and the absence, from the organized polities of the world, of any essential social liberty or culture, throws the individual back upon himself. For himself and in himself he can rediscover the secrets of faith, of hope, of happiness." (John Cowper Powys.)

Many other moderns, who either subscribe partially or not at all to the philosophy of the cult of personality, hold that the supreme end of man is the prosperity, progress and culture of the human race. Some unite this end with the good of the individual and others subordinate the individual to the social good. They conceive the human race as a certain absolute entity, subordinate to no one and purely terrestrial, and they substitute the race for God. This ideal of prosperity or of terrestrial culture may be called *humanism.* The term humanism signifies nature, human dignity, the development of nature to its highest perfection. In the minds of some humanists the term has gradually attained a meaning contrary to Christian truth, and is now used to signify man, both the individual and especially the race and its progress, as emancipated from an eternal destiny. Thus Paulsen writes: "A perfect human race is the supreme good and the last end." It is to be noted that this false philosophy of human destiny is frequently contracted to signify "nationalism," which holds that the progress of one's own nation is the highest good.

It needs no great mental effort to apply these false principles to many pernicious movements which are active in our midst to-day—nudism, eugenic sterilization, contraceptive birth-control, communism, and some forms of Fascism. All these in some way or another are reducible to the principle of the autonomous man, whether considered as an individual or as the race.

TOPICS FOR DISCUSSION

1. Why must beatitude consist in some activity and not, v.g., in the *Nirvana* of Schopenhauer?
2. Why cannot the physical essence of beatitude consist solely in the operation of the will?
3. What other operations possibly exercised by the beatified do not enter into the state of beatitude essentially?
4. Why must the operations by which the intellect and will possess God be perfect?
5. Why cannot the senses be apt and destined for the possession of God?
6. What kind of proportion between human nature and the Divine nature is necessary for beatitude?
7. How are different degrees of beatitude possible?
8. Explain why the order of an animal's being is not violated by its destruction at the hands of man.
9. Show the difference between natural and supernatural beatitude.
10. Do the intrinsic and extrinsic *ends of the work of the will* coincide?

THESIS V

The relatively ultimate intrinsic end of man in this life is such an exercise of volitional activity as will prepare and dispose him for his final state of perfection and beatitude.

Explanation of the Thesis

42. It is evident, supposing the truth of our thesis, that two possibilities are eliminated: first, that beatitude is attainable in this life; secondly, that beatitude is attainable neither in this life nor in the next. Our justification for so wording the thesis lies in what has already been proved. It has been demonstrated in the preceding pages that beatitude consists in the perfect knowledge and love of God. We have only to consult our own experience and the testimony of others to know that such a state is never attained so long as we are in this life. Moreover, beatitude and the pres-

ence of evil are inconsistent; wherefore our final end cannot be reached in a life beset by sickness, misery and death. In the words of a classical author, the whole terrestrial life of man is summed up in eight words: "Men are born; they suffer, and they die." As to the second possibility, it is removed from consideration by the simple argument that, since beatitude must be attainable and is never possessed in this life, it must be attainable hereafter.

Proof of the Thesis

If the attainment of the final perfection of man is dependent upon the character of his volitional activity in this life, then the relatively ultimate intrinsic end of man in this life is such an exercise of volitional activity as will prepare and dispose him for his final state of perfection and beatitude.

But the attainment of man's final perfection is so dependent.

Therefore, the relatively ultimate intrinsic end of man in this life is such an exercise of volitional activity as will prepare and dispose him for his final state of perfection and beatitude.

Proof of the Major:

Evident from the concepts of relatively and absolutely ultimate ends.

Proof of the Minor:

(1) Inasmuch as man is free in his volitional activity, if an act tends to perfect him, its contrary or contradictory will tend to degrade him. By the perfective act, he tends towards final perfection; by the degrading act, he recedes from it.

(2) The dignity and nature of man demand that the attainment of his final perfection should depend upon his volitional activity in this life. God moves creatures to their ends in accordance with their natures. Irrational creatures are physically impelled by Him, but man cannot be physically necessitated and still remain free. Man must *freely* seek his end. A *free* and *deliberate self-direction* of man towards his final end is impossible unless he can fail to reach it, and hence the attainment of man's final end must be dependent upon his volitional activity in this life.

(3) The wisdom of God demands that possession of Himself through beatitude should not be forced upon man, as if it were a thing of no value, but should be granted as a reward for proper volitional activity.

Scholia

43. Man's absolutely ultimate intrinsic end is not an end *absolutely* to be attained. It is *conditioned* upon the proper use of his free will. Man's *absolutely* ultimate extrinsic end, i.e., God's glory, is *absolutely* to be attained and will be achieved by all creatures.

44. It is impossible to distinguish in this life two relatively ultimate ends of volitional activity: one primary, which is the pursuit of the last end; the other secondary, which consists in a moderate prosperity in the present life. All ought to be a means to the attainment of blessedness and God's glory.

TOPICS FOR DISCUSSION

1. Why are we justified in stating that man's final end is to be attained hereafter?
2. If God is all-powerful, why does He not *make* man attain his absolutely ultimate intrinsic end?
3. Does not your reply to the last question leave you with the unsatisfactory alternative that man, by deliberately failing to attain his final end, can defeat God's purpose in creating him?
4. Show why a free and deliberate self-direction of man towards his final perfection is a method of attainment consistent with the wisdom of God?
5. Why is it impossible to distinguish two relatively ultimate ends of volitional activity?

READINGS FOR CHAPTER IV

Adversaria Ethica, Brosnahan.
Catholic Encyclopedia, "End of Man," vol. ix, p. 582; "Highest Good," vol. vi, p. 640.
Glenn, "Ultimate End of Human Acts," p. 56.
Ross, "The End of Man," chap. 3, p. 44.
Poland, "Perfect Happiness," chap. 2, art. 3, p. 26.
Leibell, "The Highest Good," p. 171; "The Last End," p. 174; "Happiness," p. 182.
Cronin, "Of the Ends of Human Action," chap. 3, pp. 46-88.
Holaind, "Teleology, or Moral Causation," first lecture, pp. 17-37.
Keane, "Human Happiness," chap. 1, pp. 11-25.
Rickaby, "Of Happiness," chap. 2, pp. 3-27.

CHAPTER V

THE CONSTITUTIVE NORM OF GOODNESS

45. We have now answered the first question which is prompted by the consideration of the Ethical Fact, viz., are some actions in reality right and good, others wrong and evil? With the end of man demonstratively established, we can now unhesitatingly answer: those actions are right and good in virtue of which man tends towards his last end, those are wrong and evil in virtue of which he recedes from his last end. The second question we proposed for examination was: what is it which *makes* an action good in itself and hence tending towards the last end, and what is it which makes an action evil in itself and hence receding from the last end?

The question of the goodness of an action has to do with its suitability to the *nature* from which it proceeds. If an action is suitable or becoming to a nature as a unitary whole or to some faculty in due subordination to that nature, it is really good and perfective of the nature. If it is really perfective of the nature, then in virtue of the action the nature must tend to its last end. We have already seen that natures are principles of operation, imitations of some perfection in God, in virtue of which a created entity is capable of eliciting operations which are imitations of Divine operations. Hence an operation which is an expression of a nature as a specific and unitary whole must be suitable to that nature, perfective of it, really good, and hence tending towards the final perfection of that nature. Such is the reason why the action of the hydrogen atom is suitable to it and good, whilst any other operation would be unsuitable to it and bad. Hence the measure and standard of any nature's operations is *proximately* that nature itself. Applying this norm to man's volitional activity, we say that any volitional activity on the part of man is suitable to him, really good, and perfective of his nature, which is in conformity with man's nature as a specific and unitary whole. This is equivalent to saying that the real goodness of any volitional action is constituted by its relationship of *conformity* to rational human nature as a unitary whole. An action is really bad if it has a relationship of *difformity* with rational human nature as a unitary whole. So much we demonstrate in the following thesis.

THESIS VI

The proximate norm of real goodness in man's volitional activity is rational human nature looked at adequately, i.e., in itself and in all its essential relationships.

Explanation of the Thesis

46. *Good* is that which satisfies desire. The power to satisfy desire involves a relation between the appetite seeking satisfaction and the object affording it. The fitness of the object to satisfy a need constitutes its goodness or suitability. Good, therefore, is that which is suitable.

Perfective good is that which is suited to supply an absent perfection or to remove a present imperfection. The attainment of perfective good by a conscious faculty necessarily involves a concomitant *delectable good,* which consists in the subjective satisfaction experienced by the faculty upon the removal of a need which has disquieted it.

Useful good is a means to the attainment of perfective good.

Perfective good may be either *real* or *apparent*. It is *real* when it is suitable to the unitary nature as such or to some faculty in due subordination to the unitary nature. It is *apparent* when it is suitable to some faculty out of due subordination to the unitary nature.

Hence we say, in summing up, that the *right* in volitional activity is that which tends towards man's absolutely ultimate intrinsic end, and the *good* in volitional activity that which tends towards his *supreme* good. Now, inasmuch as man's last end is also his supreme good, the right and the good in man's volitional activity are identified, i.e., whatever volitional actions tend towards man's last end as his supreme good are *good*. The further question, to be solved in this thesis, concerns the principle which *makes* actions so tend, which *makes* actions suitable to man's nature and hence *really good*. This is the question of the constitutive norm of goodness.

47. A *norm* is a standard or measure.

A *proximate* norm is the standard or measure nearest the thing to be measured.

An *ultimate* norm is the standard or measure upon which a proximate norm ultimately depends, and from which it ultimately draws its efficacy.

Rational human nature looked at adequately is rational human nature considered according to its essential intrinsic and extrinsic orders. Intrinsically and essentially we find in man an order of subordination of his vegetative to his sensitive, and of his sensitive to his rational life.   Extrinsically and essentially we find man a *contingent* being with a relationship of dependence upon God, a *social* being with a relationship of equality with his fellowmen, and a *proprietary* being with a relationship of stewardship over irrational beings as their extrinsic end.

Proof of the Thesis

48. The proximate norm of real goodness in man's volitional activity is the measure or standard nearest the actions in question which determines whether or not the actions are perfective of man as a unitary whole.

But the measure or standard nearest volitional actions which determines whether or not they are perfective of man as a unitary whole is man's nature looked at adequately, i.e., in itself and in all its essential relationships.

Therefore, rational human nature adequately considered is the proximate norm of real goodness in man's volitional activity.

Proof of the Major:

Evident from the definition of a norm and of real goodness.

Proof of the Minor:

Natures are principles of action.   Hence it is rational human nature, from which volitional activity immediately proceeds, which proximately determines whether or not a particular action is in conformity with itself as the eliciting subject.   Moreover, rational nature must be considered *adequately,* i.e., according to its essential intrinsic and extrinsic orders, because only thus is it regarded as a unitary whole.

Corollary

49. Any volitional action, therefore, which is in conformity with the intrinsic and extrinsic orders of man's nature is an action really good.   On the contrary, any action which is in positive conflict with these is *really* bad, although it may be *apparently* good. For it is only by being in conformity with rational nature *adequately considered* that a volitional act possesses the property of expressing man's nature as a unitary whole.

Scholion

50. An action proceeding with deliberation and free will, i.e., freely with knowledge of the action's relationship to the norm of real goodness, is a *moral* action, because such an action is distinctively human and constitutes man's customary mode of action.   It is good or bad morally in so far as it is elicited with knowledge of its *conformity* or *non-conformity* with the norm of real goodness. Morality, therefore, as applied to a volitional act, consists in a quality which comes to the act in virtue of its being elicited with knowledge of such conformity or non-conformity. Hence instead of speaking of the real goodness or badness of volitional action we may now refer to its *morality,* and instead of speaking of the norm of real goodness and badness we may refer to the *norm of morality.*

TOPICS FOR DISCUSSION

1. What question does the thesis on the good in volitional activity purport to answer?
2. What is the constitutive norm of goodness in volitional activity?
3. In what does the real goodness and badness of volitional activity consist?
4. Define good. What relation does the concept of good involve?
5. What is the difference between useful good and perfective good?
6. Is an apparent good necessarily a good in some sense? Why?
7. What is the intrinsic essential order in rational human nature? The extrinsic essential order?
8. How is a volitional act placed in the classification of morality?
9. Why may we speak of the norm of morality instead of using the term, "norm of real goodness and badness"?

THESIS VII

The ultimate norm of real goodness in man's volitional activity is the Divine nature.

Explanation of the Thesis

51. The ultimate norm of real goodness in man's volitional activity is the last norm upon which the proximate norm depends, and the reason why the proximate norm is just what it is. It is therefore the original measure of all that is measured by the proximate norm.

Since the proximate norm of real goodness in man's volitional activity, as we proved in the last thesis, is rational nature looked at adequately, and since that nature proceeds by creation from God, it is evident that the ultimate norm is found somewhere in God. According to our way of thinking about God, we make distinctions between God's nature, His intellect and His will. The question in the thesis is, whether morality ultimately depends on God's nature, or on His intellect, or on His will, according to the mental distinctions we make in God. Occam, Gerson, Descartes and Puffendorf hold that all moral distinctions arise exclusively from the free will of God. We say that the ultimate norm is the Divine nature.

Proof of the Thesis

52. The ultimate norm of real goodness in man's volitional activity is the last reason assignable why rational nature adequately considered is precisely what it is.

But the last reason assignable why rational nature is precisely what it is is God's nature as distinct, according to our way of thinking about God, from His intellect and from His will.

Therefore, the ultimate norm of real goodness in man's volitional activity is the Divine nature.

Proof of the Major:

From the definition of ultimate norm it follows that, that is the ultimate norm which is the last reason assignable why human nature, the proximate norm, is just what it is.

Proof of the Minor:

God's free will, in its creative activity, is dependent on and is guided by His Divine intellect according to our way of thinking about God. According to the same way of thinking, the Divine intellect does not make its object, but presupposes it and that object is the Divine nature. Hence in the act of Divine creation God's will is dependent upon His intellect and God's intellect is dependent upon the perfections of the *Divine nature* as imitable in the external order.

TOPICS FOR DISCUSSION

1. What is the meaning of the term "ultimate norm of real goodness or of morality"?
2. Could God arbitrarily determine by His will all actions of man as good or bad?
3. If the answer to the second question is negative, what is the reason?

THESIS VIII

The concrete determinants of morality are the object of the volitional action, the end of the agent, and the circumstances.

Explanation of the Thesis

53. *Generic* goodness depends upon the relationship of *conformity* between volitional actions and rational human nature as the objective norm of morality. Nevertheless, man as an actual being becomes subjectively good by reason of eliciting individual moral acts. Nothing in the concrete is merely generic; neither are man's moral acts, i.e., they are good or bad in a definite, specific way.

Moral acts are *generically* good or bad in the same way, viz., they are in conformity or out of conformity with the objective norm of morality. But *specifically* an act of almsgiving differs from an act of justice, just as an act of thievery differs from an act of murder. In other words, there are various species of good acts, likewise of evil acts. Our question in this thesis is: what is it in concrete volitional activity that determines its conformity or non-conformity with rational human nature in such wise that volitional acts differ specifically among themselves? We answer the question in a series of propositions.

First, however, we must again distinguish between interior acts and exterior acts. By interior acts we mean acts elicited by the will and completed within that faculty. All other acts of a volitional nature are exterior or commanded. With regard to *interior* acts we shall treat (A) of their goodness, (B) of their wickedness and (C) of their indifference. Thereafter we shall turn our attention to *exterior* acts.

A.

(1) The Interior Act Receives Its Specific and Essential Moral Goodness from the Object of the Act.

We do not aim to demonstrate that the interior act receives *some* goodness from the object, for it is evident that it does from what has been said of the norm of morality. Rather we are concerned with what constitutes the volitional act in a certain species of moral goodness, e.g., justice. It will be proved that it is so constituted by the formal object which moves the will in any particular volitional act.

Proof

54. A. Every act is specified by its formal object. The same, therefore, must hold true in the case of the morally good act.

B. An act of justice is in such a species of virtue, because it has for its object the preservation of the strict right of another and is thereby distinguished from other virtues with different formal objects.

Scholion

55. The same act of the will cannot have two species of moral goodness, because it cannot have two different formal objects and still remain an individual act.

(2) The Interior Act Receives from the Circumstances an Intrinsic but Accidental Goodness.

Circumstances, as understood here, are adjuncts which modify an act already constituted in a certain species of goodness. They may be either *objective,* by reason of affecting the object of the act, or *subjective,* by reason of affecting the act regarded in itself.

56. *Proof* (by examples) : To give $100 in alms is better in itself than to give $50; to love God more intensely is better than to love Him less intensely.

(3) The Interior Act Receives from the End of the Agent an Extrinsic and Accidental Goodness.

(1) The question here is of the end of the agent, not of the object of the act.

(2) It is unnecessary to demonstrate that an act with an evil object can never become good in virtue of the *purpose* of the agent.

(3) It is evident that an act indifferent as regards its object can receive goodness from the end of the agent.

57. An act of the will can have a relation to its object in two ways : (A) The motive reason for wishing the object may be for some further end, in which case the goodness of the act is totally from the end of the agent and the act itself solely a means to the further end; (B) the will may wish the object *as a good in itself* although with reference to a further end.

Proof

58. Suppose the case that you wish to honor God and for this reason determine to give alms. Your intended action is specifically an act of almsgiving, but is also extrinsically an act of religion. In other words, it is commanded by the virtue of religion, although elicited by the virtue of mercy.

B.

(1) Malice Is Not a Positive Entity.

Proof

59. The act, in so far as it is positive, tends towards some object under the formality of good, for it is impossible to intend an evil act under the formality of evil. Now precisely under this aspect, i.e., that of being a positive entity, a moral act cannot be evil and from this argumentation it follows as a consequence that malice is not a positive entity.

> N.B.—God is certainly the cause of any positive entity and hence of any act to the extent that it falls under this classification. Being infinitely good, He cannot be the cause of moral malice; and malice, therefore, cannot be a positive entity.

On this point St. Thomas says: "Every act, in as far as it has some being, in so far has goodness; but in as far as it is wanting somewhat in the plenitude of being, which is due to a human action, in so far is it deficient in goodness and so is said to be evil." 1, 2, Q. 79.

(2) Malice Is a Privation of the Rectitude Due to Human Nature in Its Activity.

Proof

60. Malice is opposed to goodness. The latter, we have already learned, consists in the conformity of the act to rational human nature adequately considered. Malice, therefore, consists in the opposite quality, i.e., the privation of such conformity.

(3) Hence Malice Is Specified Proximately by the Moral Goodness to Which it Is Opposed and Remotely by the Object, in as far as the Object Is out of Harmony with Rational Human Nature Adequately Considered and as Such Is Willed.

Proof

61. Privations differ among themselves according to the difference between the goods of which they are privations. Malice, therefore, is similarly differentiated. Moreover, goodness itself is specified by the object of volitional activity and malice consequently is remotely specified by the object, because the object willed is out of harmony with rational nature in a particular way.

Scholion

62. Like goodness, malice can be modified by the circumstances and by the end of the agent. But there is in this matter a wide divergence between goodness and malice. Evil circumstances add a new species of malice to the evil act in addition to the species of malice it already possesses from its evil object, and the same is true of an evil end of the agent. For example, there are three species of malice in the act by which the will determines to steal a sacred object in order to commit murder. On the contrary, a good act is capable of possessing but a single species of goodness.

C.

A Morally Indifferent Individual Act Is Impossible

63. Having shown the difference between good and evil interior acts, we come to the question as to whether the division is adequate. Can there be, in other words, interior moral acts which are neither good nor evil, but indifferent?

A volitional act may be considered in the *abstract,* purely according to the object by which it is specified, i.e., in a state of precision from the end of the agent and the various circumstances, or it may be considered in the *concrete,* together with the end of the agent and all the circumstances. No one disputes that there are actions *indifferent* in the abstract. There are many actions interior and exterior, e.g., walking, studying, which considered in themselves and purely according to their objects are neither in positive conformity with rational human nature nor in positive conflict with it. With regard to the indifference of volitional acts in the concrete there is a difference of opinion. The one maintained in this thesis is that of St. Thomas.

Proof

64. We readily grant that a volitional act may be indifferent in the abstract. For such an act, however, to be indifferent in the concrete, it must be so not only in its object and in its circumstances, but also from the point of view of the end of the agent. This latter is impossible, and so a morally indifferent individual act is also impossible.

The proof of the implied minor is as follows: Since useful good has not the characteristic of being an end, the end of the agent in every volitional action must be either a moral good or an apparent perfective good out of conformity with the nature of man as man. But in the first supposition the action becomes morally good from the end of the agent; in the second, morally bad. For man ought always to act as man, viz., as a rational entity, and not as a brute for *mere* sensual delectation. In the case of man the use of what is delectable is not regulated by instinct, as in the case of brutes, but by intellect.

Scholion

65. In the use of delectable things an actual intention referring them to the real good of man is not required. If the use is ordinate, such use tends by its own weight to the good of man as man, hence to his real good, hence to his moral good.

D.

Exterior Acts Are Morally Good or Bad Only by Extrinsic Denomination from the Elicited Acts by Which They Are Commanded.

Proof

66. Exterior acts cannot be formally moral because they are not formally free. The elicited act of the will *is* formally free, whereas exterior acts, e.g., the lifting of an arm, the bending of a knee, are the results of elicited acts of the free will, prior to themselves.

TOPICS FOR DISCUSSION

1. Can a concrete human act be merely generically good?
2. What gives a concrete volitional act its *specific* and *essential* goodness?
3. What do we mean by the specific goodness of a concrete volitional act?
4. Could a morally good volitional act have more than one essential species of goodness?
5. Do the circumstances of an act contribute to its intrinsic or to its extrinsic goodness?
6. Do circumstances add to an act intrinsic specific goodness?
7. Could the end of the agent add to an act *essential* specific goodness?
8. If malice is not a positive entity, does it follow that there is really no evil?
9. Could you define a morally evil act as an act deprived of the rectitude due to human nature in its activity?
10. If God is a co-operating cause in all human activity, does it follow that He is a cause of an evil act?
11. Can an evil volitional act be in more than one species of malice at the same time?
12. Could the concrete act of playing ball on the front lawn of the Fordham campus be morally indifferent?
13. Could the external act of killing another be in itself morally good or bad?

THESIS IX

There are actions which are morally good or evil intrinsically.

Explanation of the Thesis

67. It is a matter of common consent that there are actions which, indifferent in the abstract, become morally good or evil because of the command or prohibition of legitimate authority. This thesis presses the question further and asks whether or not there are some actions which, independent of such a command or prohibition, are by their very nature morally good or bad.

We have seen that an action receives its specific moral goodness or badness from its object. This object may be in such positive accord with the nature of man that its alternative is out of harmony with the same. An action with such an object is said to be *intrinsically* or *of its very nature* good. Likewise the object of an action may be such that it is neither in positive accord nor in positive discord with human nature, wherefore we denominate the action itself *intrinsically* or *of its nature* morally indifferent. Such an act becomes either good or bad by reason of the circumstances or of the end of the agent. Again, the object may be positively out of accord with rational human nature, and in this case the action is said to be *intrinsically* or *of its nature* morally evil. In all cases of determining the positive conformity or difformity between the objects of actions and rational human nature, care must be taken to consider the latter adequately.

68. The adversaries of this thesis are the moral positivists, who deny that the distinction between good and evil actions is based upon the nature of those actions. They affirm that the difference is based upon some *extrinsic* reason such as law or custom. The following are the theories advanced by these ethicians:

(1) Hobbes and Rousseau declare that those actions are good which are commanded by the state and those evil which are prohibited by the state.

(2) Comte, Lévy-Bruhl, Paulsen and others teach that moral distinctions depend upon the grade of evolution, on education, on custom and on practice.

(3) Evolutionists teach the notions of moral good and evil are the result of the evolution of man's social life.

(4) Occam, Gerson, Descartes and Puffendorf hold that all moral distinctions arise exclusively from the will of God.

Proof of the Thesis

69. Actions are morally good or evil intrinsically or of their very nature whose objects are in positive accord with rational human nature or in positive discord with the same.

But there are actions whose objects are in positive accord with rational human nature or in positive discord with the same.

Therefore, there are actions which are morally good or evil intrinsically or of their very nature.

Proof of the Major:

The specific nature of an action depends upon its object. Consequently an action whose object is by its nature in accord with human nature is of its nature or intrinsically good as regards its morality.

Proof of the Minor:

The minor may be proved by examples. The worship of God is positively in accord with rational human nature looked at adequately, whereas blasphemy is in positive discord with it.

Scholion

70. As is evident from all that has been said heretofore, "Independent Morality," or the theory that moral distinctions have no dependence whatsoever upon God, is an absurdity. Morality is definitely based upon order in the universe, order upon the natures of things, and the natures of things upon the Divine Essence.

71. *Erroneous Opinions of Philosophers on the Norm of Morality.*

The innumerable false opinions of philosophers with regard to the norm of morality can be reduced to these systems:

(1) Utilitarianism

Under this name can be grouped all the systems which hold that the morality of an act consists in its *utility* as a means to the attainment of some good. From the diversity of the good to be obtained we derive the different species of *Utilitarianism:*

A. *Private Utilitarianism,* which is also called *Sensualism* or *Hedonism,* teaches that the end of this life consists in the greatest felicity or pleasure of the agent, and hence that actions are good or bad as they promote or diminish this felicity or pleasure. If the action brings both pleasure and pain, either remotely or proximately, one must examine which effect is more pronounced. This doctrine was held by Aristippus, Epicurus, Democritus, among the ancient moralists, and among more recent ones, by Diderot, Helvetius and Feuerbach.

Democritus (460-370 B.C.) taught that the means to felicity was virtue, which renders us independent of cupidity and external things, with the result that we have need of very few things and can rightly discern between the pleasures to be sought and those to be avoided.

Aristippus, Cyrenaicus (435-354 B.C.), was the first to teach pure Hedonism. The supreme good, according to him, is pleasure and that the present pleasure of the body. The sum of all pleasures of the individual body constitutes felicity. Any pleasure is good, even though it may be obtained by the most debased action. Nothing, of itself and by its nature, is good or evil. Virtue is only good as a means to pleasure.

Epicurus (341-270 B.C.). From him Hedonism received the name of Epicureanism. He placed the highest felicity in the absence of pain and in the greatest amount of pleasure, whether corporeal or spiritual. The principal virtue is the right discernment of pleasures. For not every pleasure is good, because it sometimes brings with it greater pain. The virtuous and wise man, therefore, is the one who rightly discerns between pleasures and pains so that in the whole course of his life he obtains a maximum of pleasures and a minimum of pains. Gassendi (1592-1655 A.D.)

revived Epicureanism and it was altogether restored in France by the Materialists and the Sensualists. Thus Helvetius (died 1771) taught that man in all his actions should solely seek pleasure and avoid pain. Virtue should be subservient to pleasure and self-denial is a sin unless it proximately or remotely increases pleasure. Similar doctrines were held by de Lamettrie, Holbach and others.

B. *Social Utilitarianism,* or *Eudæmonism* or *Altruism* makes common felicity the norm of morality. Actions are, therefore, good or bad in as far as they promote or impede the common felicity. The more an action promotes the common good the better it is; whilst the more it impedes it the worse it becomes. This system was developed by *Puffendorf* following in the footsteps of Cumberland. Puffendorf does not admit an intrinsic and necessary difference between good and evil, just and unjust, but he makes that difference depend ultimately on the *free* will of God. Granted, however, this free decree of God, the difference between good and evil, just and unjust, remains fixed. The Creator placed upon the nature of man the law of sociability so that all actions which are in conformity with the law of sociability and the common good are themselves good, whilst those which are repugnant to these are evil. Among the more recent philosophers who held this system are the Positivists as, Comte, Littré and many others, as John Stuart Mill, H. Sidgwick, H. Lotze and F. Paulsen. This opinion makes the felicity of the human race, or the progress of culture, the supreme end of man. The supreme law, according to *A. Comte (1798-1857),* is to live for all humanity. Hence *Altruism* became the name for *Social Utilitarianism* or *Eudæmonism* which puts the supreme end of man and the norm of morality in the greatest felicity of the human race. *G. Wundt* does not wish the common felicity to be the end of the moral order, but the progress of culture itself.

C. *Herbert H. Spencer* tried to devise a system which would reconcile Social Utilitarianism and Hedonism when he applied to Ethics the theory of evolution. Actions which are simply good are those which increase life or, what is the same thing, bring pleasure without any mixture of pain. But to-day, because of the imperfect evolution of the human race and its imperfect adjustment to social conditions, private and common good are often in conflict, and consequently one good ought to be subordinated to the other. Therefore, to-day an absolutely good method of activity is not yet possible, but various compromises ought to be made between Altruism and Egoism. However, in the process of evolution men will more and more conform themselves to social conditions so that their egoistic inclinations and tendencies will be perfectly subservient to the common good. After this period of evolution and adaptation, any one, by following his egoistic inclinations, will necessarily promote the common good and then there will be perfect harmony between Egoism and Altruism so that *goodness will be absolute not relative* as it is to-day. Then there will be possible an absolute ethic which will deduce, a priori, from principles of evolution, infallible rules for the moral life of man. If one should ask how it will come to pass that Egoism will be reconciled more and more with Altruism, the answer is that this will happen through sympathy, the tendency of which will be to make altruistic actions more and more pleasurable.

D. *Negative Eudæmonism.* A. Schopenhauer (1788-1860), the father of our modern Pessimism, believed that positive felicity is impossible and that felicity only consists in the absence of misery and pain. He holds that the existent world is the worst possible world and full of misery. Hence he infers that the supreme end of man is the denial of the will to live and that this denial is principally attained by asceticism. Whilst the world exists the end of the moral order can be nothing else than to diminish misery by compassion. Good actions are those which proceed from pure compassion without any egoistic motive.

E. *Social Progressiveness* is the system which calls good whatever promotes culture, science and art.

F. *Private Progressiveness* is the system which calls those actions good which promote the perfection of the agent. This is the doctrine of the schools of Leibnitz and Wolff.

(2) Intuitionalism

All the followers of this system agree that the difference between good and bad is derived from a certain intuition, as it were, of some faculty. If it is asked of them why a certain action is good or bad, they answer, because some faculty affirms it in virtue of an immediate intuition. There are three divisions of this school:

A. *Moral Sensism,* which starts with the assumption of a *Moral Sense* distinct from the intellect by which we have, as it were, an intuitive apprehension of what is good and what is evil. This is the opinion of Anthony Shaftesbury, Hutcheson and others.

Anthony Ashley-Cooper Shaftesbury (1671-1713) tried to erect his whole scheme of ethics on the affections of the soul. He distinguishes the following kinds of affections or inclinations: Sympathetic or Social, Egoistic and Non-natural. Besides these sensual affections there exists a rational affection consisting in an esteem of the beautiful and the good and in a contempt for what is base. Virtue consists in the harmony of these affections or in their correct ordination so that all, either proximately or remotely, are subordinate to the good of the species. Non-natural affections are always bad, and egoistic ones only when they are at variance with the social affections. This harmony of the affections gives pleasure to the moral sense which is the instinct of nature. The doctrine of Shaftesbury on the moral sense was developed further by *Francis Hutcheson (1694-1746)*. The good is pleasing to this sense, the bad displeasing, and for this reason we feel an attraction to good and an inhibition with regard to evil. *Thomas Reid (1710-1796)* held that the common sense of man was the ultimate norm of morality. All men instinctively assume certain principles as true without being able to give any reason for their truth.

The moral sense, according to the opinion of the Moral Sensists, performs the function of conscience. Certain things are pleasing to it, others displeasing, the first are good, the latter evil. Nevertheless, many adherents of this school, if one considers the objective reason of the distinction between good and evil and not the method of knowing it, in reality belong to the school of Social Utilitarianism. And the reason is this, since the moral sense which they assume does not make the morality of the act but only perceives it and performs the function of a subjective criterion, it is necessary to press the question further as to what is the ultimate objective reason for the distinction between good and evil. To this question they answer that the reason is found in the perfect harmony of man's egoistic inclinations and his social ones. According to them, therefore, actions which proceed from social benevolence and desire for the common good are themselves good, whilst actions are evil which proceed from egoism, since this is repugnant to the common good.

B. *Fr. Herbart (1776-1841)* assumed as the norm of morality a certain Moral Taste. He thus made ethics a part of æsthetics. The moral value of the will according to Herbart does not depend upon the objects with which it is concerned, but only on the relation of the various volitions to each other. Some volitional relationships immediately give pleasure, others displeasure. In this way certain practical exemplary ideas originate in us which are the norm of morality both for individuals and for society.

C. *Moral Rationalism.* According to Kant the categorical imperative of autonomous reason is the supreme norm of morality. Immanuel Kant (1724-1804), in his *Critique of Pure Reason,* came to the conclusion that metaphysics properly so-called was impossible. We have indeed sensible intuitions of things in space and time, but space and time are merely subjective sensible forms; what the things are in themselves we cannot know. These empirical intuitions are the objective element or the material of our knowledge, the subjective and formal element are mere subjective forms of the intellect by which we ascribe to the material element a certain form of quantity or quality, of existence, of causality, etc. Thus we come to synthetic, a priori judgments.

Reason, finally, orders the concepts offered to it by the intellect according to the three ideas of the Ego, of the world and of God. These cognitions of the intellect and of reason are merely subjective without objective value.

Scientifically, therefore, and by *theoretical reasons* we cannot arrive at a knowledge of things outside of ourselves. However, Kant believes that *practical reason* leads us to faith in God and immortality in the following manner. He begins from those things which conscience testifies to all men with regard to the moral order. From the common sense of men nothing is *simply good,* except good will, which has value in itself, independent of exterior things, for instance, riches, talent, etc. What is this good will? Not that which is led by a eudæmonistic principle or that which seeks some empirical end, i.e., one known from experience. Such ends, as Kant supposes, are all sought because of sensitive and egoistic motives, which are altogether contrary to true morality. But that will is good which does *what* the moral law commands and solely *because* the law commands it. A will which does not act from a motive of duty has indeed legality, but not morality. For true morality there is required conformity between the law which we observe and the *"maxim,"* that is, the principle or subjective motive for which we observe the law. Moreover, because a moral law is universal and has validity for all rational beings, the *"maxim"* can only be good and right if it has the capacity to receive a form of universal law, or, as Kant himself declares, "If I can wish that my maxim become a universal law." In other words, my action is bad, if I cannot wish that any one else in the same condition can place the same action because of the same motive.

Practical reason (which according to the doctrine of Kant is identical with the will) is called pure because it is independent of matter and regards solely the form of universality. One acts morally only when he is motivated by pure reverence for the law, not when he is moved to activity through love of some good known by experience. From which we may infer that *autonomy* is essential to morality, i.e., that the will observes its own proper law. In the *heteronomy* by which we subject ourselves to the law of another, we are always led, according to Kant, by a eudæmonistic motive of love, of hope, of some good or fear of some evil. For this reason Kant calls our *practical reason* legislative. The *practical reason* is a law and an end in itself. The universal and absolute form by which it legislates is called the *categorical imperative,* so as to distinguish it from *hypothetical imperatives,* which only command conditionally, v.g., if you do not wish to beg in old age you must labor in youth.

On this moral doctrine Kant bases three *postulates* of practical pure reason, viz., three truths which, on the supposition of the moral order, must be accepted and believed, but which cannot be scientifically proved. These three truths are liberty, immortality and the existence of God. Law postulates liberty (we *ought,* therefore we *can.*) Besides, the necessary object and end of the created will is *to effect the supreme good.* But this good embraces a dual element: sanctity or absolute conformity with moral law and beatitude corresponding to this sanctity. This sanctity can never be fully attained by any creature nor the consequent perfect beatitude. Hence Kant concludes that the destiny of the created will consists in this that it should perpetually tend towards unlimited sanctity. But this perpetual progress supposes the perpetual existence or the immortality of the soul. Finally, there must be present a cause which can unite to sanctity its proportioned felicity, and this cause is God. Outside of this we can know nothing about God. He is not to be conceived as a legislator or as a judge. Any worship of God except rectitude of life is valueless and abominable.

TOPICS FOR DISCUSSION

1. Are there actions which are morally good or evil because of the command of legitimate authority?
2. Does the specifically moral goodness or badness of a volitional action depend upon its object?
3. Are there some objects which are always in positive accord with human nature adequately considered, and other objects always in positive discord with it?
4. What do you mean by an action intrinsically good?
5. What would be the result if God could arbitrarily by His will determine the goodness or badness of all actions?

REFUTATION OF FALSE DOCTRINES WITH REGARD TO THE NORM OF MORALITY

THESIS X

Utilitarianism, which declares temporal felicity, either private or public, to be the norm of morality, is false.

Proof of the Thesis

72. That doctrine with regard to the norm of morality is false which (1) makes man an end in himself, and (2) makes the norm of morality inconstant and variable.

But Utilitarianism which teaches that temporal felicity, whether private or public, is the norm of morality is such a doctrine.

Therefore, Utilitarianism which teaches that temporal felicity, whether private or public, is the norm of morality is false.

Proof of the Major:

As the philosophers determine different ends to be attained by volitional activity and as the norm of morality assigned by them differs with the difference of ends, so a system which determines man himself to be the end of his volitional activity must necessarily assign a false norm of morality. For we have seen in Chapter III that the absolutely ultimate extrinsic end of man's volitional activity is God's glory. Hence a system which assigns man himself as the end (i.e., absolutely ultimate) of his volitional activity and therefore the utility of an action for advancing man's temporal felicity, whether private or public, as the norm of morality is false. In Thesis IX we proved that there are actions which are morally good or evil intrinsically and hence independent of places, times, circumstances and persons.

Proof of the Minor:

Utilitarianism, whether private or public, makes temporal felicity the end of man's volitional activity and hence makes man an end in himself. Temporal felicity, whether private or public, is necessarily an end inconstant and variable. It will be inconstant and variable with differences of time, place, circumstances and persons.

THESIS XI

The norm of morality assigned by Moral Sensism is false

Proof of the Thesis

73. The norm of morality assigned by Moral Sensism, whether it be material or spiritual, is inconstant and variable, and besides is not connatural for the specific act of a rational being.

But the norm of morality cannot be inconstant and variable and must be connatural for the specific act of a rational being.

Therefore, the norm of morality assigned by Moral Sensism is false.

Proof of the Major:

The Material Sensists assign an organic sense as a means of distinguishing between good and evil through sensible attraction to good or sensible aversion from evil. Thus, Rousseau, Schopenhauer and others. The Spiritual Sensists assign a spiritual sense as a means of distinguishing good from evil through the natural attraction or aversion to good or from evil. Thus, Shaftesbury, Hutcheson, Adam Smith and Jacoby. It is evident that this blind attraction and aversion, whether sensible or spiritual, will vary with difference of time, places, circumstances and persons. It is also evident that such attractions and aversions are not connatural for the specific act of a rational being, since the connatural attraction of such an act implies the intellectual perception of good or evil as such.

Proof of the Minor:

In Thesis IX we have proved that there are certain actions intrinsically good and bad and hence constantly and invariably so, because independent of time, places, circumstances and persons. A moral act is a specific act of a rational being; it is a volitional act and hence dependent upon free will under the guidance of deliberate reason.

THESIS XII

The Moral Stoicism of Kant is false

Proof of the Thesis

74. That system is false which (1) assigns the ultimate norm of morality as something merely subjective; (2) which excludes from the sphere of morality many actions evidently good, and (3) which is at variance with human nature as constituted by its Creator.

But the Moral Stoicism of Kant is such a system.

Therefore, the Moral Stoicism of Kant is false.

Proof of the Major:

The Major is clear (1) because we proved in Thesis VII that the ultimate norm of morality is necessarily the Divine Essence; (2) because any sound system of morality cannot exclude actions which are evidently good, and (3) because a true system of morality cannot be at variance with human nature as constituted by its Creator.

Proof of the Minor:

By way of preamble, it ought to be noted that the moral doctrine of Kant presupposes his doctrine on synthetic, a priori judgments in the speculative order already refuted in Logic. For the categorical imperative in the practical order is such a judgment, in which the practical reason unites, a priori, the idea of absolute obligation with an empirical action or element. Therefore, Kant's whole system collapses with the rejection of his synthetic, a priori judgments. Nevertheless, we will prove the minor by reasons strictly moral.

(1) Kant teaches that the merely subjective, autonomous reason through the categorical imperative commanding or forbidding is the ultimate norm of morality. These decrees of autonomous reason either have objective validity or not. If they have, by that very fact a further norm is demanded and the autonomous reason is not the ultimate norm. If the autonomous reason is merely subjective, the consequences can be illustrated by the supreme Kantian law: "So act that the maxim of your will can always become an objective principle of universal legislation." How can it be determined when the maxim of the will can be a principle of universal legislation and when it cannot be such a principle? If independently of the objective order one ought to determine this for himself, the difference between good and bad depends on the subjective judgment of the agent, and there is lost that "absolute value" of the formal foundation of morality which Kant boasts that he has established. If it is determined from the objective order, the norm of morality is independent of autonomous reason.

(2) Kant teaches that action alone to be morally good which is placed purely from reverence to the law and because the law commands. Therefore, an action ceases to be morally good which is placed out of reverence for the law, but at the same time with a mixed motive of pleasure. Likewise, such heroic actions as are not commanded by the law, e.g., the rescue of another at the risk of one's own life, cease to be morally good. But this is contrary to the common opinion of men to which Kant makes appeal for proof of his exclusive norm of morality.

(3) We have proved that the ultimate felicity of man is essentially connected with the internal perfection of human nature. Therefore, man cannot tend towards his *deontological* end without at the same time tending towards his *felicity* which is, therefore, a true end of human activity by an ordination of the Author of Nature. But a system which exacts the positive exclusion of this *eudæmonistic* end that an action may be morally good is at variance with human nature as constituted by its Creator.

TOPICS FOR DISCUSSION

1. Does the norm of morality assigned by different systems depend upon the end assigned to volitional activity?
2. What do you mean by utilitarianism?
3. Does utilitarianism assign a eudæmonistic or deontological end to volitional activity?
4. What do you mean by intuitionalism?
5. What are the three kinds of intuitionalism?
6. Is Kant's "practical reason" an intellectual faculty?
7. What does Kant mean by "autonomous reason"?
8. Does Kant make man himself the end of volitional activity?
9. Does Kant make the end of volitional activity deontological or eudæmonistic?
10. In our system of Ethics is the end of man deontological or eudæmonistic?

READINGS FOR CHAPTER V

Adversaria Ethica, Timothy J. Brosnahan, S.J.

Ethica Generalis, Joseph Donat, S.J.

Philosophia Moralis, Victor Cathrein, S.J.

Catholic Encyclopedia, "Egoism," vol. v, p. 328; "Hedonism," vol. vii, p. 287; "Cyrenaic School," vol. iv, p. 591; "Epicureanism," vol. v, p. 500; "Altruism," vol. i, p. 369; "Utilitarianism," vol. xv, p. 251; "Benthamism," vol. ii, p. 482.

Glenn, "Morality of Human Acts," chap. iv, pp. 97-120.

Ross, "The Norm and Criteria of Morality," chap. iv, p. 60.

Turner, "From Kant to Our Own Time, Third Period," pp. 528-653.

Leibell, "Utilitarianism," p. 375; "Altruism," p. 380; "The Kantian Ought," p. 383.

Cronin, "The Moral Criteria," chap. v, pp. 124-174; "On Kantian Formalism," chap. ix, pp. 256-274; "On Hedonism," chap. x, pp. 275-317; "Of Utilitarianism," chap. xi, pp. 318-371; "Evolution and Ethics," chap. xii, pp. 372-441; "Ethics of Transcendental Evolution," chap. xiii, pp. 442-471; "The Moral Faculty," chap. xiv, pp. 472-505; "Of Intuitionism," chap. xv, pp. 506-536.

Holaind, "Utilitarianism," 5th lecture, p. 117-151.

Keane, "The Moral Criteria," chap. iv, p. 46; "Utilitarianism," chap. v, p. 55.

CHAPTER VI

MORAL OBLIGATION AND MORAL LAW

Introduction

75. In the beginning of our exposition of Ethics we set before ourselves three questions, suggested by the Ethical Fact, to be investigated and answered. The first concerned the reality of the distinction between right and wrong, good and bad in volitional activity. The second had to do with the norm which constitutes this difference. Both questions have now been adequately answered. There is an objective and intrinsic difference between at least some good and bad volitional actions. The generic goodness and badness of an action consists in its relationship to the norm of morality, whereas its concrete goodness or badness is constituted by the concrete determinants of morality, i.e., by the object or the end of the action, the circumstances, and the end of the agent.

The norm of morality which we have established is a constituent norm, viz., it constitutes either *generically* or *specifically* the morality of an act. It has reference to the intellect and guides the intellect in discovering and judging the moral qualities of volitional activities in virtue of which they are designated as good or bad, right or wrong. The necessity which this norm imposes is of itself only *logical*, viz., it binds the intellect in virtue of truth. It is now time to inquire about the norm which binds the will, or about the norm by which man not only as *rational* but also as *free* is bound. The *necessity* of this norm extends itself to man as possessed of reason and free will, viz., to the whole man as man. It binds him *practically* and is called the *complete* norm of human activity. This norm is either *subjective,* as *synteresis* and *conscience,* or *objective,* as *eternal, natural* and *positive law.*

Our third question in examining the Ethical Fact was in relation to the concept of duty, or the consciousness of the absolute, though not physically compelling, necessity to do good and avoid evil, which is also a deliverance of the Ethical Fact. We wish to know whether man has the duty or the unconditioned moral obligation to direct his volitional activity in such wise that he will do good and avoid evil. The answer to this question will be found in a consideration of moral law, eternal and natural.

Moral law may be defined, in accordance with St. Thomas, as: "An ordination of reason for the common good by him who has care of the community, and promulgated." It is said to be:

A. "An ordination of *reason,*" because it is a rule of action *existing in the reason.* It is the property of law to order actions to a given end, and to order to an end belongs *directively* to reason, which judges of the end and of the means to it. Furthermore, law is said to be something of reason, because it ought to be conformed to right reason. Law is the rule of moral actions with regard to their rectitude. Such a rule of rectitude cannot be law unless it is itself right and reasonable.

B. "An *ordination* of reason," because it efficaciously or with a certain kind of necessity moves the subject towards the end proposed, inasmuch as it obliges the subject to obey. Law has its efficacy from the will of the superior. To order to an end belongs *directively* to the reason, but effectively to the will, which imparts motion towards the end. By its efficacy, law is distinguished from counsel, which imposes no necessity, but merely attracts the will by the proposed good.

C. "*For the common good,*" because law always implies order *for a community,* which it directs with reference to an end, the common good. In this respect it differs from precept, which is imposed not upon the community, but upon an individual or a group of individuals.

D. "*By him who has care of the community,*" because to order to an end belongs to him in whose care the end is. Therefore, since law is the ordination of a community to its own end, the common good, to make a law is a right belonging either to the whole community or to the entity which has care of the community.

E. "*Promulgated,*" because law is a rule by which subjects are moved to an end by the superior. But rational and free beings cannot be moved to an end by a rule in accordance with their natures, unless the rule be applied to them by manifestation to their intellects. Consequently, this manifestation or promulgation is necessary. Therefore, since the law is imposed upon the community, it must be promulgated to the community by authoritative denunciation.

76. Moral law may be considered in a threefold state: (A) In the mind of the *legislator;* (B) in the minds of the *subjects* to whom it is promulgated; (C) in some *external sign* by which it is conveyed to the subjects. Law in the first state is law *actively* considered, in the second, law *passively* considered. The third formality of law is not necessary for the perfection of every kind of law, as will be evident from what we have to say about the Natural Law. Law looked at *completely* is law considered both actively and passively.

Many acts on the part of the superior are required for law *actively* considered: (A) Judgment, by which he understands that a certain rule is right and convenient for the community; (B) *willing,* by which he wishes to oblige his subjects to the observance of the rule; (C) *reason,* by which he directs this act of the will to his subjects and which is called *command.* Law formally consists in this last act, but essentially supposes the act of the superior's will from which it draws all its efficacy.

Moral law, as above defined, must be carefully distinguished from the moral laws improperly so-called of which there was question in Epistemology. In the proper sense, moral laws are dictates of the practical reason by which the superior intimates his will to the subject. These have no influence upon the will save in so far as they are known. The moral laws of Epistemology, e.g., no one lies gratuitously, are merely certain constant modes of human activity consequent upon the free determination of the will, hence they neither command nor prohibit.

77. Law is divided according to its effects into law of *command,* law of *prohibition, permissive* law and *punitive* law. Law of command is called *affirmative,* inasmuch as it induces to the performance of certain acts. Law of *prohibition* is called negative by reason of requiring the omission of certain acts. *Permissive* law is thus denominated, not only because of the denial of obligation with regard to the action in question, but also because of the positive will of the legislator that this act be permitted. In virtue of such permission there is always an obligation not to impede in their pursuit of the law those to whom permission is granted. *Punitive* or *penal* law is given this name because it aims to bring it about that physical punishment be inflicted on the transgressor of the law.

78. Law is classified with respect to its duration as *eternal* law and *temporal* law; with respect to its immediate author as *Divine* and *human* law; with respect to its foundation and mode of promulgation as *natural* and *positive* law. Positive law is again subdivided into Divine and human, and this latter into *ecclesiastical* and *civil.*

THESIS XIII

There exists in God an eternal moral law

Explanation of the Thesis

79. There is question here of law looked at *actively,* i.e., in the mind of the legislator. So considered, a law in the mind of God must necessarily be *eternal.* As we have already seen, law actively considered implies a variety of activities on the part of the

lawgiver. Care was taken to emphasize the fact that law in this respect formally consists in the act of *command* or *"imperium."* Hence St. Thomas defines law *actively* considered as: "Nothing else than a dictate of practical reason in the ruler who governs a perfect community."

80. We have learned from the postulates of Ethics and from the earlier theses that the *common extrinsic end,* hence the common good, of man is God's *extrinsic glory.* This, in turn, is perfectly realized by the attainment of man's *intrinsic end, beatitude,* by the perfect knowledge and love of God. Now, this final perfection of man is the product of volitional activity in accordance with its proximate norm, rational nature adequately considered, by which man observes the natural order of things. In virtue of His infinite wisdom, and holiness or love of order, God cannot be indifferent to man's realization or non-realization by his free activity of this natural order. On the contrary, He must direct and move him to his natural end. This He does by law, and this law looked at *actively* is *eternal* moral law. Hence the accuracy of St. Augustine's definition of the Eternal Law: "The intellect and will of God, commanding the observance of the natural order and forbidding its disturbance."

Proof of the Thesis

81. A moral law is a promulgated ordination of reason for the common good by him who has care of the community.

But in God there is such an ordination, promulgated from eternity.

Therefore, there is in God an eternal moral law.

Proof of the Major:

Evident from the definition of moral law.

Proof of the Minor:

A. The ordination or dictate of reason, which is an essential element of moral law, implies, first of all, that the lawgiver *knows* a rule of conduct right and suitable for his subjects. Of a certainty God, Who knows the natures of things as imitations of His own nature, is aware from eternity of activities right for the attainment of the ends of created natures and suitable for the perfection of these natures.

Secondly, the ordination of reason supposes an act of the governor's will whereby he *wills* to bind the subjects to the right and good rule of conduct. In virtue of His infinite wisdom and holiness, God assuredly wills to bind men to that volitional activity which is right and good for them and without which they cannot attain the intrinsic and extrinsic ends of their natures, i.e., cannot realize the natural order of things.

Thirdly, the ordination of reason necessarily involves the command or *"imperium"* by which the governor *directs* his will to the subjects. It would unquestionably be at variance with the infinite attributes of God uselessly to evoke the former two requisites of moral law, and then to omit the act in which moral law actively considered formally and essentially consists.

B. This dictate of reason is for the *common good* of God's rational subjects, because the attainment of one and the same intrinsic and extrinsic end is the good common of all men.

C. This dictate of God's reason is that of *one who has care of the community,* because God is the ultimate cause, the conserver, the co-operator, and the last end of man. Hence man is wholly dependent upon God and is entirely in His care.

D. This dictate of the Divine reason is *eternal,* because, as Theodicy teaches, God is purest act and all His activity is identical with His essence. Hence God is absolutely immutable and there can be no change in Him.

E. This dictate of reason is *promulgated* from eternity. However, it was not *terminatively* promulgated until the actual creation of man. Such *terminative* promulgation is essential to law *passively* considered; it is also essential to law *actively* considered, if the lawgiver be human, because a human lawgiver may change his mind in the interval elapsing between his determination to enact the law and its application by external sign to the superior's subjects. With God, on the other hand, no change of mind is possible. As a consequence, the dictates of reason in question are promulgated from eternity, in the sense that as soon as man was created the law was *passively* promulgated without any change in God.

Scholion

82. St. Thomas defines the Eternal Law as: "The plan of the Divine wisdom, according as it is directive of all acts and motions." In its widest sense the Eternal Law directs all motions, even those of irrational beings, to their appointed ends. Properly speaking, however, the plan of the Divine wisdom is called law only in so far as it is referred to the direction of rational beings and imposes on them *moral obligation.* A more accurate discussion of this famous definition of St. Thomas will be illuminating. St. Thomas calls the Eternal Law:

"A *plan*," because "plan" means the practical reason *ordering* and implies two things: *in the intellect* an *exemplary* plan of the actions and motions of all created entities; *in the will* an act, efficacious of itself, commanding the acts and motions suitable to the nature of each entity. This plan differs from *governance,* which is the actual and continuous direction, or determination, physical or moral, of those acts and motions. *Governance,* therefore, is the execution of the law.

"*Of wisdom,*" because it is the act of God operating in virtue of His knowledge of the cause and the being caused, and of the proportion and efficacy of acts and motions as means to an end. The plan we are considering directs all things through their acts and motions to the common end of the universe.

"Of the *Divine* wisdom," because only in Divine wisdom is there knowledge of the adequate nature described above. The power, physical and moral, requisite for such direction to the common end of all things, and also the necessity of such direction, is proper to God. For on the supposition of the decree of creation, the direction of all acts and motions to this end is a consequent necessity.

"*According as it is directive,*" because the Divine plan involves not only an exemplary idea of things to be created and the direction of the Divine operation itself, but also the direction of the created entity acting and moved. Furthermore, this latter direction operates not only intellectually but principally by determination, i.e., by *physical* determination in the irrational entity and partially also in the rational entity, and by *moral* determination only in the rational entity.

"*Of all acts and motions,*" because it controls, guides and regulates every operation in every creature, and all to the common end of the universe.

The Eternal Law in its adequate concept allows neither exception nor dispensation. It is absolutely *universal,* because God knows from eternity all things that are to take place and He has His own reasons why He permits each. Hence, when He permits anything against the physical laws of nature, the permission does not contravene the Eternal Law, because in the latter law the exception is already provided for. Likewise the permission on the part of God of anything contrary to the moral law postulates a reason in the Divine mind for the allowance. The Eternal Law, therefore, contains or has reference to everything which takes place, but in different ways. For this reason it is absolutely universal, admitting of no dispensation and of no escape to any created entity. And so with respect to actions morally bad, there is in the Eternal Law the compensation of a natural penalty for the violation of the natural order and of a supernatural penalty for the violation of the supernatural order, just as in it there is a reward for morally good actions.

All law is derived from the Eternal Law in so far as the obligation to obey comes ultimately from the Eternal Law.

The Eternal Law, just as any other law, is affirmative or commanding, negative or forbidding, permissive and punitive.

TOPICS FOR DISCUSSION

1. What element in the Ethical Fact is being investigated and validated by the present chapter?
2. Define moral law and explain each term in your definition.
3. What are the three formalities under which moral law may be considered?
4. What acts on the part of the superior are required for law actively considered?
5. Are the moral laws we consider in any way different from the moral laws discussed in Epistemology?
6. Give the divisions of law with respect to its effects. With respect to its duration.
7. Under what formality do we consider moral law in the present thesis?
8. Defend St. Augustine's definition of the Eternal Law.
9. How are the three acts required on the part of the superior for law actively considered fulfilled in the case of the Eternal Law?
10. Why is the Eternal Law for the common good of its subjects?
11. Why is the Eternal Law a dictate of reason by one who has care of the community?
12. Why is it eternal?
13. How has it been promulgated?
14. State and explain St. Thomas' definition of the Eternal Law.
15. Why can there be neither exception nor dispensation with regard to the Eternal Law?
16. Whence does all law, Divine and human, natural and positive, derive its binding force?
17. Does the Eternal Law permit of division according to its effects?

THESIS XIV

There exists in man a Natural Moral Law

Explanation of the Thesis

83. We are concerned in this thesis with the Eternal Law *passively* considered, i.e., as promulgated and existing in the minds of its subjects. Since God guides all creatures to their appointed ends primarily by their natures, which are principles of operation, the Eternal Law must be promulgated by the very nature of man. It is thus by its method of promulgation distinct from all positive Divine law. The Eternal Law looked at *passively* is, therefore, called the Natural Law and is defined by St. Thomas as: "The participation in the Eternal Law by the rational creature." This participation must be according to the specific nature of man, hence by reason. It is by human reason that God directs and moves man to his intrinsic and extrinsic ends, just as he leads irrational entities by physical law.

84. Since it is by *reason* that man is led by God and leads himself to the fulfilment of his part in the plan of creation, reason must have the *native capacity* and the *impulse* to form those practical obligatory judgments with regard to good and evil, i.e., with regard to the necessity of doing good and of avoiding evil, which are a reflection or promulgation of the intellect and will of God commanding that the natural order be observed and forbidding its disturbance.

85. We have said that reason must have the *native* capacity and impulse to *form* such judgments. According to Psychology, there are no innate ideas—consequently the ideas of good and evil, and practical judgments of conduct, such as, good is to be done and evil avoided, are neither *innate* ideas nor *innate* judgments. What we mean by "the native capacity and impulse" to form such ideas and judgments is this: just as every human faculty has the native capacity and impulse to perform under proper conditions the activity for which it is designed, so the human intellect, under the conditions proper and necessary for its activity, has the native capacity and impulse to form the ideas and judgments which are the first principles of conduct. These principles, because they are the result of such a capacity and impulse, are a promulgation of the Eternal Law. Just as the intellect has a tendency to form the ideas and judgments which are fundamental to the whole order of speculation, so it has a similar tendency to formulate the ideas and judgments which are basic to the whole order of conduct.

86. Inasmuch as the capacity and impulse to formulate the first principles of human conduct are bound up in the nature of the intellect by God precisely for this purpose—that through the natural fulfilment of this capacity and impulse the Eternal Law may be promulgated or exist *passively* in the minds of its subjects—the capacity and impulse may itself be called in a certain sense *a participation in the Eternal Law by rational creatures.* This participation in the Eternal Law is the Natural Law looked at *virtually,* so denominated because it is in virtue of it that the rational creature, acting according to the laws of reason and under the conditions necessary for its exercise, formulates the practical moral judgments which specifically promulgate the Eternal Law.

As a matter of fact, St. Thomas calls this very capacity and impulse Natural Law, when he describes the Natural Law as: "The light of intellect, given to us by God, in virtue of which we know what must be done and what must be avoided." Indeed, Cathrein says: "It is essential to the Natural Law that it should be a manifestation of the Eternal Law inseparable from the existence of man, a divinely impressed, natural, *innate* inclination towards the acts proper to him." It should be noted, however, that through the deficiency of the proper conditions practical judgments of conduct may never be formed in individual cases.

87. Provided that reason is sufficiently developed and provided it has formulated the truths fundamental to the speculative order and also, however untechnically, the ideas of real (moral) good and evil, then the practical reason, in virtue of this capacity and impulse, formulates the first principles of human conduct, i.e., good ought to or must be done, order ought to or must be observed; evil ought to or must be avoided, disorder ought to or must be omitted. From these first principles the practical reason formulates other universal principles of conduct which flow from them with obvious inference, such as, God ought to be loved, blasphemy ought to be avoided, justice ought to be observed, injustice ought to be avoided. These practical judgments or principles of conduct, formed as a result of the native capacity and impulse spoken of above, are *dictates of the human reason* with regard to the right and the wrong, the good and the bad in human conduct. They are the Eternal Law looked at passively, or the promulgation of the Eternal Law. As dictates of the human reason, directing and impelling man to the common good in virtue of the impression given to man's intellect by the Supreme Lawgiver, they are themselves *law*. These universal, practical, obligatory dictates of human reason, by which man knows that he is bound to the performance of good and the avoidance of evil actions, are the Natural Law looked at formally, i.e., according to its specific nature.

88. Hence we may define the natural moral law as: a rule of action, mandatory in form, which reason itself discovers, as having been established by the Author of man's nature and promulgated by being imbedded in the nature of man. With regard to this definition it ought to be noted that a rule of action for moral beings may be made known: (a) through the use of reason; or (b) through some external sign, oral or written, given by the maker of the law. Since the Natural Law is promulgated by the very nature of man, it is distinct from positive law, which is promulgated by some external sign, oral or written. Natural Law is distinct from a physical law of nature because the binding power of Natural Law is *moral necessity*, while the binding power of physical law is *physical necessity*.

89. It is our task to prove in this thesis: (A) That God necessarily stamped the human reason with a capacity and impulse to form universal, practical and categorical judgments of conduct, or that the Natural Law exists *virtually* in the human reason; (B) that this capacity and impulse is necessarily fulfilled under the conditions required for the proper functioning of the intellect, or that the Natural Law exists *formally* in the human reason.

Proof of the Thesis

90. There must exist in man by nature a participation of the Eternal Moral Law.

But this participation of man by nature in the Eternal Moral Law implies: (a) A Natural Moral Law looked at *virtually,* and (b) under proper conditions a Natural Moral Law looked at *formally*.

Therefore, there must exist in man by nature a Natural Moral Law.

Proof of the Major:

God *must* apply His decree of direction and motion to the natures of all created things. For the natures of things are principles of operation by which entities, in virtue of an interior principle, tend towards their proper ends. Without this participation in the Eternal Law natures would not have that which is necessary to attain their ends.

Proof of the Minor:

This participation of man by nature must be a participation according to his *specific nature,* hence by his *intellect*. It implies:

A. A *Natural Law looked at virtually*. For it implies a capacity and an impulse to formulate obligatory principles of conduct. Without this capacity and impulse, man's reason would be by nature *indifferent* to whether or not it supplied man's will with direction and impulse towards its specific and ultimate end. The will would be ordered by nature to attain beatitude by its volitional activity, but the intellect upon which it depends for direction and impulse would not be ordered by nature to lend this altogether necessary help. Hence man's specific nature would be wanting in what is strictly necessary for the attainment of his last end. Since this is an impossibility, there must be in man's intellect a capacity and an impulse to formulate practical, obligatory judgments with regard to conduct which will supply direction and motion to the will. This is what we mean when we say that there is in man a Natural Law looked at *virtually*.

B. A *Natural Law looked at formally.* Every natural faculty, under the conditions proper for its operation, will produce its proper effect. Hence the capacity and inclination of the intellect to give direction and impulse to the will through practical, obligatory judgments with regard to conduct will, under proper conditions, be fulfilled. These judgments will be: (1) *Universal,* because the specific tendency of the intellect is towards universal truth; (2) *practical,* because they are judgments with regard to conduct; (3) *dictates of reason,* because they give to the will natural *direction* by showing it what is good and what is evil, and *motion* by showing it the necessity of doing the good and avoiding the evil. Hence they are judgments imposing obligation or *dictates of reason.* They are, moreover, *for the common good,* inasmuch as they give direction and impulse towards man's intrinsic and extrinsic ends, which are the common good of the universe; *by Him Who has care of the community,* for they are formulated in virtue of a capacity and an impulse implanted in reason by the Author of Nature; and *promulgations* of the Eternal Law, because by them there exists in the minds of God's subjects a knowledge of the Eternal Law.

Since, therefore, these judgments are practical dictates of reason for the common good by Him Who has care of the community and promulgated, they are *law looked at formally,* i.e., according to its proper definition, and *Natural Law,* i.e., law whose mode of promulgation is through nature; for Natural Law is a rule of action mandatory in form which reason itself discovers, as having been established by the Author of Nature and promulgated by being imbedded in the very nature of man.

Corollary

91. We have proved absolutely by *a priori* reasoning that God is bound so to construct the human reason that it will, with ease and facility, formulate practical, obligatory judgments with regard to conduct. These judgments give *direction* and *motion* to the will towards its ultimate end, and are *dictates of reason,* viz., are a promulgation of the Eternal Law or of the intellect and will of God commanding the observance of the natural order and forbidding its disturbance. A consideration of human history in all its variety and phases ought, therefore, to give us *a posteriori* verification of the fact of a participation by rational nature in the Eternal Law. At the very outset of our consideration of Ethics, we called attention to the Ethical Fact, viz., that men have at all times judged that some actions are good and some actions are bad and that there is an obligation to do the good and to avoid the bad.

These judgments which constitute the Ethical Fact are a deliverance of the consciousness of the race. They are *constant* and *universal,* and we have now given the only possible solution for their constancy and universality. Men have constantly and uniformly judged that there is a difference between right and wrong in human conduct and that there is a categorical obligation to do the right and to avoid the wrong, because man's reason has been stamped by the Author of Nature with a capacity and an impulse so to judge under the conditions proper for the exercise of this capacity and inclination. Nothing can explain the constancy and universality of these judgments except a cause as constant and universal as the judgments themselves. Obviously this cause only can be the human reason.

We have proved, therefore, the objective validity of the elements of the Ethical Fact. The first question raised by the Ethical Fact was this: Is there *de facto* an objective difference between the good and the evil in human conduct corresponding to the judgment of such a difference contained in the Ethical Fact? We answered that there is. We established the absolutely ultimate, intrinsic end of man and concluded that those actions are good and suitable to the nature of man which lead towards man's last end or beatitude really to be attained, those bad and unsuitable to the nature of man which lead away from this end.

In considering the Ethical Fact we next asked ourselves: What makes a volitional act good? In reply to that question we declared and proved that a volitional act is constituted good and hence tending towards man's last end by its conformity with rational human nature looked at adequately, i.e., in itself and in all its essential relationships.

Finally, our investigation of the Ethical Fact led us to ask: Is man *de facto* obligated to the performance of good and the avoidance of evil actions, as he subjectively judges himself to be? We answered this question by showing that God, in virtue of His infinite wisdom and sanctity, must and *de facto* does oblige man by the Eternal Law to the performance of good and the avoidance of evil actions. We further showed that this Eternal Law has been promulgated in man's specific nature, existing there *virtually* by a capacity and impulse to formulate practical and obligatory judgments of conduct, *formally* by universal dictates of reason made when the conditions proper for the normal functioning of reason are at hand. God was hypothetically necessitated to promulgate His Eternal Law in the nature of man. That promulgation terminates racially, so to speak, in the Ethical Fact. If the judgments contained in the Ethical Fact are not true, God has not promulgated the Eternal Law, a consequence which is an absurdity.

Scholia

92. The author of the Natural Law is God, the means of promulgation is the reason of man, the subject is man himself, but the command or *moral determination* is placed immediately upon the will. What is the Natural Law looked at comprehensively? Before answering this question fully, we again call attention to the fact that God has gifted man with the faculty of reason. In this faculty, as connatural to it, He has placed an innate, necessary *tendency* to formulate practical, obligatory, moral judgments. The necessity of making these judgments arises from their *objective evidence,* whether immediate or mediate. Examples of such judgments are: Good must be done, evil must be avoided; parents are to be loved, nothing is to be stolen. With regard to *immediate* evidence in the practical moral order the following is to be noted: The speculative precedes the moral order, and the first principles of reason which are immediately evident to us belong to the speculative order. Hence, when we speak of *first principles* in the moral order, we do not exclude but presuppose certain principles of the speculative order, of which some are immediately evident and others mediately evident in that order. With these principles already known, the first principles of the practical moral order are immediately evident. God has also bestowed upon man a rational will, together with a connatural tendency to obey these practical moral judgments. The inclination, however, leaves unimpaired the physical freedom of the will to resist this tendency and not to obey the practical moral judgments.

With the foregoing understood, we proceed to answer our question: What is the Natural Law looked at *formally* or *in itself?* The Natural Law looked at formally or in itself consists in practical, universal, obligatory, moral judgments. *Virtually* considered, the Natural Law consists in the faculty of reason. *Fundamentally,* the Natural Law consists in the objective evidence for the practical, universal, obligatory, moral judgments. This evidence is found in rational human nature looked at in itself and in all its essential relationships.

93. The Natural Law differs from the Eternal Law because:

(A) the Eternal Law is law *actively* considered; the Natural Law, law *passively* considered;

(B) the Eternal Law is *eternal;* the Natural Law *temporal;*

(C) the Eternal Law is Divine in a very special sense by reason of being *in* God; the Natural Law Divine by reason of *proceeding* from God;

(D) the Eternal Law is extended to *every* creature; the Natural Law limited to the *rational* creature;

(E) the Eternal Law is the *ultimate* complete rule of morality; the Natural Law the *proximate* rule of morality.

94. The Natural Law differs from positive law because:

(A) the proper and immediate matter of the Natural Law is activity *intrinsically* promoting or frustrating the end to be effected by man on earth; such matter in positive law is also activity which does *not intrinsically* promote or frustrate that end;

(B) the Natural Law is *necessary;* positive law *free;*

(C) the Natural Law proceeds from *God* as the Author of Nature *immediately;* positive human law from *man immediately* and mediately from God.

(**N.B.**—Positive Divine law, although coming immediately from God, proceeds from Him as the Author of Grace);

(D) the Natural Law is necessarily directive of *all* men; positive law is *not* necessarily directive of *all* men;

(E) the Natural Law is *immutable;* positive law *mutable;*

(F) the Natural Law proceeding as a necessary act of the Divine will is manifested only by *nature* and the *human reason;* positive law is manifested by some *external sign.*

95. The Natural Law differs from *moral conscience,* because the Natural Law consists in universal judgments, whereas moral conscience consists in the particular judgments by which those universal principles are applied to concrete, individual acts.

96. The proper matter of the Natural Law is activity according to its intrinsic proportion to foster or frustrate the ultimate end of the Creator. For this proportion is the basic reason why God internally wills, and consequently is necessitated to command or prohibit these human acts. Hence:

A. Every human act which is intrinsically proportioned to frustrate the end of the Creator is prohibited by the Natural Law not only *always* but *for always,* because it is impossible that such an act should not always and at every moment frustrate this end.

B. The human act which is intrinsically proportioned to promote the end in question can be of two kinds. Some acts, thus proportioned, are such that their omission necessarily frustrates the end; such acts the Natural Law commands *always* but *not for always,* because it is not necessarily true that their omission frustrates the end at every moment. Only their prolonged or perpetual omission frustrates the end. Other acts intrinsically proportioned to promote the end are such that, although their exercise promotes the end, their omission does not frustrate the end. Acts of this description the Natural Law positively permits, i.e., confers on man the right of eliciting them, provided they are elicited, at least interpretatively, because of the last end.

Consequently, an act which is forbidden is *positively* against the Natural Law; the omission of an act which is commanded is *negatively* against the Natural Law. An act which is commanded is *positively* in accordance with the Natural Law, and is said to be in accordance with the *preceptive* law. An act which is permitted is said to be in *negative* accordance with the Natural Law and in accordance with the *permissive* law. Besides, if with regard to two acts one is better than the other (in so far as it better promotes the last end), the better act falls under the admonition of *counsel*.

Finally, an act intrinsically promoting the last end is commanded because it is good, and an act intrinsically frustrating the last end is forbidden because it is bad. From this fact there appears a fundamental difference between the Natural Law and positive law. The latter often *makes* the act good which it commands, and the act bad which it forbids.

97. Since in the pursuit of the end to be effected by his activity man has by nature relations to many things, we can consider the subjection of human acts to the Natural Law according to these essential relations. Hence:

A. Certain acts have immediate reference to *God,* the last end, as the object to be glorified. Of these, those by which man recedes from God are intrinsically proportioned to frustrate the end to be effected, God's glory, and so fall under the prohibition of the Natural Law. For the end to be effected essentially involves approach to God, inasmuch as that end is totally ordered to God as the *end for which* and also involves God as the *end which* by reason of the nature of beatitude, which can consist only in the knowledge and love of God. Again, acts by which man so approaches God, that their omission involves departure from Him, necessarily and intrinsically promote the end to be effected and are commanded by the Natural Law.

B. Certain acts have immediate reference to *other men.* Those which promote the conservation of social life are intrinsically proportioned to further the end to be effected by man's activity and are consequently either commanded or permitted. Vice versa, acts which are harmful to the conservation of social life are forbidden. By giving man a social nature, God indicates that He includes in the end to be effected the production, conservation and perfective development of human society.

C. Certain acts have immediate reference to *irrational entities*. Those which use irrational entities according to their capacity to conserve and perfect human life, whether individual or social, are intrinsically proportioned to the end to be effected by volitional activity and are commanded or permitted by the Natural Law. Those, on the other hand, which use irrational entities in that manner or measure which is harmful to human life are forbidden. For God, in giving irrational entities a nature proportioned to the service of human life, manifests His inclusion of an ordinate use of these beings in the end to be effected on earth by human activity.

D. Certain acts have reference to the *body of man* and to the *inferior faculties of the soul*. Acts which direct the body and the inferior faculties towards the use and benefit of the superior and specific faculties of man, and so towards the specific unity of human nature, are intrinsically proportioned to the end and so are commanded or permitted, whereas those which aim at harm to the superior faculties are prohibited. From the fact that God gives a specific unity to human nature, we know that He includes in the end to be effected the use of everything in human nature to help the activity of the specific faculties and of the specific tendency.

98. *The Nature of the Obligation Arising from the Natural Law.*

The necessity imposed on the human will is *final* necessity, i.e., it arises from an end. This necessity implies an *absolute* reason why the commanded act must be placed, why the forbidden act must be omitted, although the physical liberty to disobey the command or the prohibition remains unimpaired. If we consider the nature of the will, such an *absolute* reason must be the *good,* mentally apprehended, which as an end is sufficient to move the will to obey the command or the prohibition.

By reason of the ordination of man to God as his ultimate end there arises a twofold final necessity:

A. A *primary* final necessity arises from the relation of man's nature to God as the absolutely ultimate end of all creatures, to whom, therefore, all other things which can be ends of human activity are essentially subordinated together with the very nature of man and all its perfections. With regard to the motivation of the will, its supreme end is that supreme, unlimited and essential good which alone adequately corresponds to the necessary and unlimited tendency of the human will. This end alone is *simply* and *essentially* necessary to the will. The human reason, therefore, understands that God is the end uniquely essential to man, that He is to be loved above all things, and preferred to every other good, and that all other goods subordinate to God are to be considered as *subordinate* in the tendency of the human will, and that every human will must be subordinated to the will of God with regard to these goods.   To act contrary to this is to depose God from the place which He necessarily has, as the ultimate end of volitional tendency in man; it is, therefore, to avert man from God as his ultimate end.   And so this is an absolute and efficacious reason why the end imposed by the will of God is to be chosen in preference to any other end which could lead the will to a way contrary to this.   This necessity of conforming my will to the will of God in order to observe in my actions the due order of my nature to God constitutes that moral bond which we call obligation.   Obligation is the proper, essential and immediate effect of the will of God commanding.   Obligation, therefore, has a relationship to the legislative will of God as to its cause.   *Formally,* however, obligation consists in the connection of my action, as it is the object of God's legislative will, with God, the supreme and necessary end of my will.

And so Obligation is defined: *The necessity of acting or non-acting, known by reason, which arises from the necessary connection of an action or its omission with the absolutely ultimate end of the human will.*

B.   A *secondary* final necessity is a consequence of the primary necessity.   It arises from the necessary connection of the action or omission with my subjective beatitude, in as far as the observance of law leads directly to this beatitude and similarly the violation of law leads to the loss of beatitude.

99.   This secondary necessity, although it is connaturally united with the commanding and prohibiting law, is not that necessity which is intrinsic and essential to this law.   The reason is because law *primarily* and *essentially* implies an order of relationship to God Himself, and its violation is opposed to the love due to God, not to the love due to myself.   Besides, the union with God which is the result of observance of law and the aversion from God which is implied in its violation, although of themselves perpetual, are predicated of the present, and not merely of the future.   The final necessity, therefore, which arises from the connection of an action or an omission with my beatitude is the proper effect of the law *sanctioned* which is a consequence of the law commanding or the law forbidding and the obligation they impose.

100.   Kant proposed the following absurdities:

A.   Man as a free rational being is an end to himself or an end in himself, not only with regard to other created entities, but absolutely.

B. Man is subjected to no law except that which his reason, in virtue of its own power, imposes on him. For reason is autonomous and its dictates deserving of absolute veneration.

C. Man is at the same time superior to himself as commanding and subordinate to himself as subject to law; he may have, therefore, a will absolutely willing and at the same time not willing with regard to the same matter.

D. Kant *feigns* God, as a "postulate of reason," not because theoretically we can have any knowledge of God, but because He ought to be something *feigned* by the mind to give force to the precepts of reason. It is reason alone which legislates; only man commands himself.

101. For the rationalists and the independent moralists, who follow Kant, human society is an immediate principle of moral obligation. The evolutionists make human nature as constituted in its present state of evolution an immediate principle of moral obligation. Kant and all of these are in agreement on this one point, that human nature is for itself the immediate principle of moral obligation and that moral obligation is altogether independent of and disassociated from any extra-mundane law.

TOPICS FOR DISCUSSION

1. Is the question of the Natural Law one of law *actively* considered or one of law *passively* considered?
2. Does God direct and move all creatures by their natures?
3. Does it follow from this that the Eternal Law must be promulgated in the natures of things?
4. Does this make the Natural Law distinct from all positive law?
5. Must man's participation in the Eternal Law be according to the specific nature of man?
6. Does God direct and move man by his reason?
7. Does man move himself by his reason?
8. If God directs and moves man by reason, must reason have the capacity and the impulse to form practical judgments with regard to good and evil?
9. Is this capacity and impulse a promulgation of the Eternal Law?
10. Does this capacity and impulse imply innate ideas and innate judgments?
11. What is the difference between the speculative reason and the practical reason?
12. Must certain judgments of the speculative reason precede any judgment of the practical reason?
13. Why do we call the capacity and impulse to form practical judgments of conduct the Natural Law looked at virtually?
14. Is it essential to the Natural Law that it be inseparable from the existence of man?
15. Does the Natural Law exist virtually in every man, whether or not he actually comes to the use of reason?
16. Describe the manner in which this capacity and impulse is exercised when a man comes to the use of reason.

THESIS XV

There appertains to the Natural Moral Law a perfect natural sanction which is not realizable in this life and which consists in the attainment or loss of beatitude.

Explanation of the Thesis

102. To sanction a law is to make it in a certain sense holy, and, therefore, so to legislate that the law may be inviolate. However, by custom, *sanction* is referred to the rewards and punishments decreed by the legislator in order that his law may be observed inviolately. Sanction can be considered *actively* and *passively; actively* looked at, it is the decree of the legislator by which he sets forth a reward for those observing the law and a punishment for its violators; *passively* looked at, it is the reward promised for the observance of law or the punishment proposed for its violation.

103. The *natural end* of a sanction is to provide efficaciously for the observance of law and consequently to uphold efficaciously correct moral order. *Primarily* this end considers preservation of order, viz., the sanction is *naturally* and *primarily* directed to the promotion of right order and to its defense from violation. This is provided for by proposing to the will an efficacious motive by which it may be induced to observe order. Under this aspect, the sanction provides for the observance of the moral order *antecedently* to the free determination of man's will. *Secondarily* this end looks to the restoration of order, the sanction, viz., intrinsically, but *secondarily,* intends the fulfilment of order according to objective justice by means of the reward and punishment which it proposes, just returns for merit and demerit. Under this aspect, the sanction provides for the restoration of the moral order *consequent* upon the evil use of human freedom.

With regard to this essential and secondary purpose of sanction as it has reference to punishment, materialists and atheistic socialists are loud in their complaints and proclaim that, "Men are to be emancipated from heaven and governed by love alone." With regard to this it must be noted that the *penal sanction* is said to be *medicinal;* first, inasmuch as the threat of punishment is a preservative medicine; secondly, inasmuch as by experience the guilty learn that punishment is attached to the violation of order; thirdly, inasmuch as by the example of punishment of the guilty others are led to the observance of order. All this indeed is not found equally in every sanction, but differently according to the different kinds of sanction. The penal sanction is also called *vindicative.* For just as the reward has an internal co-ordination with the notion of merit, so punishment has with the notion of demerit. Demerit exacts punishment from the very concept of an integrated order of justice. For the present it is sufficient to remark that it is one thing to *exact vengeance* and another thing to *vindicate* order. The punishment, therefore, is willed by the legislator *conditionally* before the guilt; after the commission of wrong, the punishment is willed *absolutely* not as an evil, but as a restoration of order, and therefore as a good.

104. There are three orders of sanctions:

(A) The *individual* order, which consists in this that all the appetites are subjected to the dictates of right reason. The sanctions of this order are: approbation and tranquillity of conscience, or its sting and remorse; integrity of soul and body, or their proper diseases; serenity of soul, or slavery to concupiscence and consequent bitterness.

(B) The *social* order, which consists in the correct observance of the relations arising from community life. The sanctions of this order are: peaceful enjoyment of the goods of life, or the loss of the same; the fruit of social prosperity, peace and happiness in domestic and public relationships, both in the temporal and spiritual order, or the consequences of social disturbance.

(C) The *universal* order, which is the moral order established in relation to the Creator and the last end. The sanction of this order is the attainment or loss of natural beatitude. This is the supreme order, which embraces as parts of itself the individual and social orders.

Moreover, since law is enacted for the common good and in behalf of the community, the sanction decreed by the legislator *proximately* and *principally* refers to the universal order, if it is a sanction of the Natural Law, and to the social order, if it is a sanction of positive human law. The sanction *secondarily* and *mediately* refers to the individual order. On the contrary, sanctions which are annexed to precepts, when the precepts are imposed for the good of individuals, *primarily* have reference to the individual order and *secondarily* to the other orders.

105. Sanction is divided by reason of its basis into *natural* and *positive* sanction. The first is based on the very nature of natural law or of the rational creature; the second is imposed by the free will of the legislator. By reason of its efficacy the sanction is *sufficient* or *insufficient,* according as it is by nature efficacious in restraining the human will to the observance of law, or has only a partial efficacy for this effect. By reason of its proportion to merit and demerit, a sanction is said to be *adequately* or *inadequately* just, in so far as it is aptly or inaptly proportioned to merit or demerit. We understand in the thesis by *perfect* sanction a sanction which is *sufficient* and *adequately* just. In the thesis, therefore, we are speaking of a *passive, natural* and *perfect* sanction, and one which has reference to the universal order. The thesis has three parts:

FIRST PART

There is a perfect natural sanction appertaining to the Natural Moral Law.

Proof of the Thesis

106. There is a perfect natural sanction appertaining to the Natural Moral Law, if its Author is holy, wise and just, and if the natural moral order must be complete in itself.

But such is the case.

Therefore, there is a perfect natural sanction appertaining to the Natural Moral Law.

Proof of the Major:

(a) If God is holy, He must will order, i.e., the observance of the Natural Moral Law; and must, therefore, will at least *some* means to that end. Hence there must be at least *some* sanction appertaining to the Natural Moral Law. (b) If God is wise, He will employ means *sufficient in themselves* to effect the observance of the Natural Moral Law; hence there must be a sufficient sanction. (c) If God is just, He will not punish transgressions of the Natural Moral Law with a penalty more severe than the evil calls for, nor will He apportion for the observance of the same law a reward less in value than the cost of the effort required to keep it. Hence there must be an adequately just sanction. Inasmuch as the same sanction has already been shown to be sufficient, the sanction is seen to be a perfect one. (d) It is obvious, that, in order to be complete and perfect, any moral order must possess its *own* sanction, i.e., must be possessed of a means proper to itself and calculated to guarantee its fulfilment. That a moral order must be complete is shown in the constant action of human legislators in establishing sanctions positive in character and incurrible in their operation to ensure the observance of the positive moral order, e.g., life imprisonment for serious crimes. A positive sanction of this kind is inappropriate to the natural moral order. Hence the sanction needed to complete the natural moral order must be natural in character and automatic in operation, i.e., must be the natural outgrowth of the law observed or the law violated.

Proof of the Minor:

(a) That God is holy, wise and just is postulated from Natural Theology. (b) That the natural moral order is required to be complete has already been persuasively indicated by our consideration of the completeness of the positive moral order, to which the moral order more immediately proceeding from God is superior. Dispensing with this argument, however, we conclude to the necessity of a natural moral order complete within itself from the fact that the Creator has seen fit to guide all things to their appointed ends by natures which are *complete* principles of operation, intended to achieve their proper ends, solely by the aid of that conservation and concurrence on the part of God, for which they have an exigency; not, on the other hand, by the help of such a *special* intervention on His part as a positive sanction would call for.

SECOND PART

This sanction is unobtainable in the present life

Proof of the Thesis

107. A perfect natural sanction appertaining to the Natural Moral Law is sufficient and adequately just.

But the sanction of the Natural Moral Law in this life is neither sufficient nor adequately just.

Therefore, a perfect natural sanction of the Natural Moral Law is unobtainable in the present life.

Proof of the Major:

Already given in the first part of the thesis.

Proof of the Minor:

(a) It is *not adequately just,* because obedience to the Natural Moral Law in this life frequently necessitates the loss of all external goods and even of life itself. (b) It is *insufficient,* because man is surrounded by enticements to sensual pleasure, for instance, wealth, honor, pride, so strong that the earthly sanctions of the Natural Moral Law, such as remorse of conscience, loss of reputation, etc., would not ordinarily avail to keep him in the path of virtue.

THIRD PART

This sanction consists in the attainment or loss of beatitude

Proof of the Thesis

108. The perfect natural sanction appertaining to the Natural Moral Law must be sufficient and adequately just, and must be the normal outgrowth of the law observed or the law violated.

But only the attainment or loss of beatitude is such a sanction.

Therefore, the perfect natural sanction appertaining to the Natural Moral Law consists in the attainment or loss of beatitude.

Proof of the Major:
Definition.

Proof of the Minor:

(a) The attainment or loss of beatitude is a sufficient sanction, for it consists respectively in the greatest good or the greatest evil conceivable for men, i.e., *perpetual* enjoyment or deprivation of the perfect good. (b) It is adequately just, for by observing the Natural Moral Law in this life, men attain the relatively ultimate intrinsic end of volitional activity, i.e., a perfect state or disposition of the will exactly equivalent to the sum total of good acts placed and evil acts avoided. Now this is precisely a preparation for the reward of obeying the Natural Moral Law, i.e., final beatitude. The same process of reasoning will show that the loss of beatitude is a penalty proportioned to the evil done in disobeying the Natural Moral Law. (c) It is a *natural* sanction, because, as we have seen, beatitude is the end or natural outcome of good volitional acts or *morally good* acts, i.e., of acts in conformity with the Natural Moral Law. Furthermore, every morally good action is a partial perfection of rational nature naturally and normally issuing into final perfection. The reverse is true of morally evil acts. (d) There is no other such sanction.

Scholion

On the loss of the last end

109. A special question arises on the perpetuity of the sanction. If we consider the premial sanction, no one who holds the survival and immortality of the soul denies its perpetuity. On the question of the perpetuity of the penal sanction the conclusion of our thesis is bitterly attacked.

The principal opponents are: (a) Those who absolutely deny that the loss of beatitude is perpetual; for they claim that perpetual punishment is in conflict with the nature of punishment and with the Divine perfections. (b) Those who do not deny that grievous sinners, unless they repent before their departure from this life, merit and *de facto* will undergo perpetual punishment They say, however, that this consists in the annihilation of the soul. In such a way, it is asserted, provision is made for right order, while the sense of humanity is not offended. (c) Others have recourse to the doctrine of probation after death. They teach that the human mind is so shrouded in darkness and the human will is so weak that it is impossible for men in this life to be guilty of a fault which would merit perpetual privation of beatitude. (d) Another opinion concedes the perpetuity of the penal sanction, but at the same time holds that this punishment will finally become tolerable on the principle that the soul by becoming accustomed to its punishment will no longer suffer. We present the following answers to these opinions:

(a) Perpetual punishment is not at variance either with the nature of punishment or the Divine attributes. Perpetual punishment would be repugnant to the nature of punishment in so far as by its nature it would be only *medicinal* and *exemplary*, but *in no way vindicative*. This, however, is untrue. For the evil of the punishment is by nature proportioned to the evil of the guilt and both of these have the same relation to each other as an *operation* by which an individual deprives himself of some form, and the privation of that form, v.g., the operation by which one blinds himself and the privation of sight. If, therefore, an individual, acting with full knowledge, full deliberation and full consent, *totally alienates himself from his last end,* the privation of this last end is by its nature perpetual. Now the natural sanction, in so far as it is *vindicative,* precisely consists in this privation as a natural consequence of guilt.

Secondly (a), the Divine attributes, with which according to this opinion the perpetuity of punishment is at variance, are *justice* and *goodness*. Perpetual punishment, it is said, is at variance with the Divine justice because there is no apparent proportion between the perpetual loss of the last end and a momentary act; it is at variance with the Divine goodness because a being infinitely good cannot love punishment. To the first difficulty we answer that some proportion must be preserved between the punishment and the guilt. This proportion, however, as is evident, cannot consist in the mere duration of the act by which the fault is committed, but must consist in the evil resulting from the act. Otherwise the criminal who killed a man by a momentary act would be guilty to the same degree as the one who by a momentary act killed the horse of the dead man. The proportion, therefore, is to be judged by the gravity of the guilt, and this by its relationship to the last end from which the one deserving of perpetual punishment totally alienates himself. It is not, therefore, contrary to the Divine justice that the one guilty of a fault should undergo the reaction of violated order, and become susceptible of punishment in the same proportion as he was guilty of disorder or sin. We answer the second argument by saying that this destroys the very concept of sanction and consequently the moral order itself. For if it is at variance with the Divine goodness to inflict perpetual punishment, when this is just, because an infinitely good being cannot love punishment, it is likewise at variance with his goodness to inflict temporary punishment. On this principle there can be no sanction for law. Besides it is not at variance with the goodness of God, that He love *order*, and consequently the means necessary for the preservation of order. "It is conceded that the punishments inflicted by God are not inflicted on account of themselves, as if God found delight in them, but on account of *something else*, viz., on account of the order that must be imposed upon creatures in which the good of the universe consists." (St. Thomas, C. G., lib. 3, c. 144.) "Hence the evil of the fault cannot come from God. God, however, can wish that the Divine good itself, or any other good beneath it, should be taken away from him who is without the capacity for it; for the good of order exacts that he should have nothing of which he is not worthy. And this subtraction of uncreated good or any other good, from the one who is unworthy, constitutes the nature of punishment." (St. Thomas, Q. D., *De Malo,* quæst. 1, art. 5.) Finally, we answer that the goodness of God is just and holy, and consequently cannot be inordinate, as it would be, if it disturbed the essential order of justice.

(b) The perpetuity of punishment cannot consist in annihilation. First, the primary end of creation is the extrinsic glory of God. But on the hypothesis of the annihilation of the soul, man by his own free will can frustrate this end. For he does not give glory to God in this world, nor can the annihilated soul give glory to God in another life. Secondly, we have already proved that the sanction of law must be efficacious. But a punishment only negatively perpetual would not be efficacious in keeping men under the restraint of the natural law and hence the primary end of creation would be frustrated.

(c) A time of probation extended beyond the limits of this life cannot be admitted. For such states of probation would succeed each other perpetually or not. If the first were true, the efficacy of the sanction and the primary end of creation would be frustrated. If the second were true, there would be an ultimate state of probation, either because the one on probation finally would repent, or because some ultimate state would be required from the nature of law. The first is gratuitously asserted; for the more one had sinned grievously and securely in the present state against the law and without punishment, so much the more freely would he act in a subsequent state under the impulse of the same nature. Thus the will to repent would be postponed from state to state of probation. This would be the end of the moral order. On the second supposition that states of probation are not to continue forever, the failure of the probationer to amend his conduct implies perpetual punishment.

(d) The punishment which consists in the loss of essential beatitude cannot become more tolerable by custom. This opinion is based upon physiological experience. Since sensible suffering becomes less vivid because the bodily organs of sensation are dulled by constant use, this opinion concludes that the same thing is true of perpetual punishment. But there is not the slightest parity between sensible and accidental sufferings and the sorrow of the soul arising from the knowledge of the loss of the ultimate end and essential beatitude. This opinion, therefore, errs on the nature of a universal sanction.

Finally, the question of the perpetuity of punishment is a question of "right" or of "fact": (a) Whether the penal sanction by its nature exacts perpetuity; (b) whether, on the supposition of the right, it would be necessary *de facto* and in every case that the punishment should be perpetual in execution. With regard to the question of "right," perpetuity is exacted from the very nature of sanction by which universal order is preserved; for this sanction must be efficacious and adequately just, i.e., perfect. Perpetuity is exacted also from the primary end of creation. The question of "fact" is a theological question. However, philosophic reason persuades us that it is worthy of a Divine legislator, infinitely wise, holy and just, that He, *de facto,* should sanction His law with a punishment which is exacted *de jure.* "Nay, this at least is arrived at as most certain on *a priori* grounds, that, granted the Divine perfections, the penal sanction can neither simply and universally be deprived of its natural perpetuity, nor even by a special intervention of the Divine mercy can its perpetuity be derogated in those circumstances, in which by that derogation the essential integrity of the purpose of a sanction would be frustrated." (Meyer, *Inst. Jur. Nat.,* vol. 1, n. 265. Cf. C.G., lib. 3, cap. 144.)

TOPICS FOR DISCUSSION

1. What do you mean by sanction actively considered? Passively considered?
2. What is the intrinsic end of sanction?
3. What does the intrinsic end primarily look to? Secondarily look to?
4. What do you mean by saying a sanction is vindicative?
5. What are the three orders of sanction?
6. What do you mean by a perfect sanction?
7. To what order does the perfect sanction primarily refer?
8. How do you show that a perpetual sanction is not against God's justice? Against His goodness?

THESIS XVI

Man by morally good actions truly merits beatitude from God

Explanation of the Thesis

110. In this thesis we solve the question which arises as to the manner in which man's morally good actions are connected with the perfect *premial* sanction of the Natural Law. In the last thesis we saw that this sanction is beatitude.

111. *Merit* in a volitional action is an exigency for a reward. *Demerit* is an exigency for punishment. This exigency, of course moral, in a volitional act, is the foundation of a moral necessity or of a moral tendency which is cognate to necessity. In man moral necessity is obligatory and arises from law. In God there can be no obligation, but a moral tendency arises because of His infinitely perfect nature. This exigency is *imperfect*, if it is the foundation not of necessity, but of a moral tendency proceeding from a counsel of law, or is the foundation of a necessity in accordance with some virtue other than justice. This latter exigency is said to be *imperfect*, because it is not the foundation of any *right* in the one who merits, although there may be an obligation in another to render a reward. The exigency is *perfect* which is the foundation of a true moral necessity or a moral tendency cognate to necessity according to *justice*. The reward is a benefit rendered because of an advantage received; punishment is evil inflicted because of detriment suffered.

112. There are two kinds of merit, *congruous* merit and *condign* merit. The first is an *imperfect* exigency for a reward; the second is a *perfect* exigency. When we say in the thesis, "man truly merits," we are speaking of *condign* merit.

113. *Condign merit* is defined as the exigency for reward founded on a moral necessity arising from some form of justice. *Objective* justice is realized when there is rendered to everyone what is his own. Objective justice is *to be realized*, when there is a relationship of equality between two persons with regard to a debt. Three things make up the nature of *justice to be realized*, *otherness, equality* and *debt*. *Objective debt* is something to be rendered to another by some one from *moral necessity*. This *justice to be realized* is perfect, if there is present a perfect notion of *otherness*, when, viz., one person is not morally the part of another or subject to his jurisdiction; when there is present a perfect notion of *equality* both between the persons themselves and between the benefit and the debt; when there is perfect notion of *debt*, viz., when the moral necessity is absolute and not merely hypothetical.

114. Among men both perfect and imperfect justice are found. There are, therefore, three forms of justice amongst men: *commutative, distributive* and *legal*. *Commutative justice* exists amongst men who are juridically equal and looks at the *arithmetical* equality of the benefit and the debt. *Distributive justice* exists between a person juridically superior and a person juridically inferior and looks at the *geometrical* equality between the benefit and the debt, viz., between the proportion of one benefit to its debt and the proportion of another benefit to its debt. Thus a ruler observes distributive justice, if, in rewarding one act of public service by a remuneration of $1,000 he rewards any public service twice as important with a remuneration of $2,000. *Legal justice* exists between persons juridically inferior and a person juridically superior, as between, v.g., citizens and their ruler.

115. Between man as the *subject* of a right and God as the *term* of a right there cannot exist perfect justice, but only imperfect. There is wanting, first, the full notion of otherness because man is a creature of God, and hence he and his belong to God. There is, however, a sufficient notion of *otherness,* because man is a distinct person whom God has made *sui juris* and to whom God has conceded a certain stewardship over himself and his possessions. There is, however, wanting between man and God the full measure of *equality,* since the persons are not juridically equal. Moreover, in the matter of merit, Divine reward is of much greater value than the good offered to God by man. There is, however, a *juridical equality* between the service rendered and the debt by the benevolence of God under an onerous condition that has been fulfilled by man. Finally, a debt with men implies moral obligation arising from moral law, whereas debt with regard to God arises from the necessity of His nature. With these limitations, implying an imperfect form of justice, we predicate *condign* merit between man and God only according to the form of *distributive* justice.

116. Furthermore, we predicate merit between man and God not *univocally,* but *analogically.* The identity appears in this that in both cases there is exigency for a reward according to some mode of justice; the diversity is apparent in this that service with men can involve either an *intrinsic* good or an *extrinsic* good; with respect to God only an *extrinsic good* can be offered to God by man. Also, the reward to be rendered amongst men can be totally alienated by him who gives the reward; God, however, always necessarily retains the supreme dominion of the reward and grants to man only a participated and subordinated dominion of the reward. Among men, finally, merit can arise according to some form of perfect or imperfect justice, according to *commutative,* *distributive* or *legal* justice; but merit with God is predicated only with regard to *distributive* and *imperfect* justice, as we have seen.

117. *The conditions of condign merit* which are *necessary* and *sufficient* are five. These, when they are verifiable with God, are modified by analogy. The conditions are:

A. *That the act of the agent meriting be free;* because merit is a consequence of imputability which implies a volitional act. An act obligatory by moral law can be also meritorious both because a sanction is necessary for the integrity of law and because obedience to law does not change the fact that the service is rendered. Such a service changes the order of equality and consequently is a foundation for a reward to be rendered in justice.

B. *That the act of the agent meriting be morally good;* because an act morally bad cannot be the foundation of a moral exigency for reward, since a law rewarding moral evil would be no law and the perfect nature of God could not necessitate reward for an evil act.

C. *That the act of the agent meriting, precisely as imputable, conferred a benefit on another;* because unless a service is rendered to another there is no change in the order of equality between two in such wise that there would be a foundation of an exigency for a reward in order to restore the equality. To fulfil this condition it is sufficient that the act of the agent should confer only an extrinsic good; besides it is sufficient that the good conferred should only be under the participated dominion of the one conferring it. Nor is it an obstacle that the good conferred, by its very nature, independent of its rendition should be under the absolute dominion of the one to whom it is conferred. The reason for this is, that the one rendering even an extrinsic service out of his participated dominion to another person, who has absolute dominion of the thing, truly acts for the good of the other and changes the order of equality as established by him who has the absolute dominion.

D. *That the act of the agent meriting be accepted by the remunerator for a reward;* because the order of equality is not formally changed unless the good really becomes the property of another, and it does not so become, unless he accepts it; and because under the condition of a reward, it does not become his property unless it is accepted with that condition. Besides, an act of one person who has no authority over another cannot be the cause of a moral necessity or of obligation on the will of another unless by his consent. There is, however, a twofold acceptance, *formal* and *explicit,* or *virtual* and *implicit.* A *formal* and *explicit* acceptance arises from an agreement or promise made under an onerous condition and manifested by a formal sign. A *virtual* and *implicit* acceptance arises when one person so acts, that, in virtue of this act, another is induced by the hope of reward to render a service to the first person. With men both kinds of acceptance may be verified; but with God in the *natural order* we predicate only *virtual* acceptance and that, indeed, with an *implicit* promise, *freely* made but with an onerous condition. By this virtual and implicit acceptance we assert that God acknowledges the acts of men and the good arising from them "for a reward," although because of the supreme dominion of God these acts already belong to Himself.

E. *That the act of the one meriting be not already rewarded through anticipation,* viz., through a reward freely accepted with an onerous condition; because, if the act has already been rewarded, then the act rendered by the agent meriting only restores the order of equality and places no new foundation of exigency.

Proof of the Thesis

118. Man, by morally good actions, truly merits beatitude from God, if the conditions for condign merit are present in these acts.

But such is the case.

Therefore, man, by morally good actions, truly merits beatitude from God.

Proof of the Major:

The major is evident.

Proof of the Minor:

(1) The action must be volitional, hence free, if it is truly a moral action. (2) The actions in question are by supposition good. (3) Morally good actions, though they confer no intrinsic benefit on God, add to His extrinsic glory. (4) God has implicitly accepted the benefit thus conferred by creating man with faculties, intellect and will, whose formal objects are unlimited truth and unlimited good. Thereby God equivalently promises man the satiation of these faculties, viz., beatitude, for proper use of these faculties by morally good actions in this life. (Cf. Theses II, III, IV and V). (5) Such actions, though not entirely unrewarded in this life, do not receive here a reward commensurate with the difficulty in placing them. This was proved in Thesis XV on the inadequacy of the sanction of the Natural Law in this life.

TOPICS FOR DISCUSSION

1. Define merit and demerit.
2. What is the difference between the natural necessity for granting a reward as it is in God and as it is in man?
3. What is the difference in man between an imperfect foundation for granting a reward and a perfect foundation?
4. What is the difference between the bases of congruous merit and condign merit?
5. Define condign merit.
6. What three elements make up the nature of *justice to be realized?*
7. Describe the three different kinds of justice.
8. By what kind of justice does man truly merit with God?
9. Is this term "merit of man with God" applied univocally or analogically?
10. What are the necessary and sufficient conditions of condign merit?
11. Show how these can find place in man's good volitional activity so as to deserve condign merit from God.

READINGS FOR CHAPTER VI

Ethica, Charles V. Lamb, S.J.

Adversaria Ethica, Timothy J. Brosnahan, S.J.

De Ethica Naturali, C. Macksey, S.J.

Philosophia Moralis, Victor Cathrein, S.J.

Catholic Encyclopedia, "Natural Law," vol. ix, p. 76; "Obligation," vol. xi, p. 189; "Duty," vol. v, p. 215; "Categorical Imperative," vol. iii, p. 432.

Glenn, "Law," art. 1, chap. iii, p. 72.

Ross, "Duty," chap. v, p. 74; "Law," chap. vi, p. 87.

Poland, "Law," chap. iv, pp. 52-75.

Leibell, "Law," part iv, pp. 301-325; "Synteresis," pp. 341-2.

Cronin, "Of Law," chap. xix, pp. 633-659; "Of Merit," chap. xvii, pp. 574-593.

Holaind, "Essence, Concrete Existence and Attributes of Natural Law," 2d lecture, pp. 37-52, 61-67.

Keane, "Moral Obligation and Natural Law," part ii, pp. 77-119.

Rickaby, part i, pp. 109-177.

Hull, the whole book.

CHAPTER VII

The Properties of the Natural Law

THESIS XVII

The Natural Law looked at in itself is intrinsically and extrinsically immutable.

Explanation of the Thesis

119. Having demonstrated the existence of the Natural Law, we now come to consider all its properties. These are: *unity, universality, immutability* and *clarity.*

Unity is a property of the Natural Law, in virtue of which, as Suarez says: "It is one in the individual man," viz., although in every man there are many precepts of the Natural Law, nevertheless all can be referred to one first principle in which, as it were, they are united, and from which the natural duties of man can be derived by reason. This property will be considered in the next thesis.

Universality is a property of the Natural Law in virtue of which, again to use the words of Suarez: "It is one in all men and in all places." That this universality is a property of the Natural Law is evident from the fact that it is a consequence, not of the reason of any particular individual, but of man's specific nature. Nor are there any difficulties with regard to this, unless those which are brought against the immutability and the clarity of the Natural Law. Hence in this thesis we treat of the property of *immutability* and in the thesis immediately following of the property of *clarity.*

120. *Immutability* is a property of the Natural Law in virtue of which it is not only the same in all men everywhere, but also the same for all conditions of persons, places and circumstances. This immutability is predicated in the thesis with regard to the law commanding and prohibiting, but not with regard to permissive law, about which something will be said in a scholion.

Change of law, or its transition from one state of determination to another, takes place when a precept or a prohibition is added to the law or taken away from it.

Intrinsic change takes place when, because of a subsequent deficiency in some essential characteristic of the law as it is looked at *significantly* or *passively,* something which was before commanded or forbidden ceases to be such. This might happen, v.g., when a precept or a prohibition of some law in the course of time no longer operates for the common good, but contrary to it, and thus becomes unjust and ceases to have an essential characteristic of law.   Here there is a question of the *deficiency* of a command or a prohibition, because no objective change can *add* to law without a new decree of the legislator.

Extrinsic change takes place by a subsequent authoritative act of some superior. In this case with regard to the Natural Law there is no question of a *precept* or a *positive* law which recalls nothing in the Natural Law; because on this supposition there takes place a mere addition of another law, while the Natural Law remains unchanged.   For it is the nature of Natural Law that it is subject to definition and perfection by positive law, as we shall see in a subsequent thesis.   Hence the question with regard to an extrinsic change of the Natural Law has reference only to the repeal of a precept or prohibition.   An extrinsic change can be brought about in three ways:

(a) *By abrogation,* if the whole law with regard to all subjects is repealed.

(b) *By derogation,* if a part only of the law is repealed.

(c) *By dispensation,* if some person is exempted from the application of the law, while the law remains in force with regard to others.

It is necessary to make a distinction between a *formal* change of law and a *material* change, which latter is not a change of law, but a change in the matter of the law.

A material change of law takes place, when, with the law remaining in full force, the human act which is its matter does not remain specifically the same by reason of which it fell under the law.   Thus a human act, which appears to be the same, because *materially* it is such, when it becomes *formally* different, no longer falls under the command or prohibition of Natural Law without any change whatsoever in the law itself.

A *formal* change of law is present when, while the human act remains *specifically* the same according to the characteristic on account of which it fell under the law, the law is changed.   In such a change the same specific act once forbidden is now *not forbidden* or vice versa, and the same act once commanded is now *not commanded* or vice versa.

A human act is *specifically* the same according to the characteristics on account of which it falls under the law, when it retains the same relation of proportion or non-proportion to the common good, not only according to all that is essential to every human act, but according to its total characteristics, arising from its object, from its circumstances and from the end of the agent.

A human act is *only materially* the same act according to the characteristics on account of which it falls under the law, either when it ceases because of some deficiency to remain a *human act,* although it remains the same physical act of man; or, when, remaining a human act, it no longer includes in its object, in its circumstances, or in the end of the agent all those elements which are the basis of its relation of proportion or non-proportion to the common good. To illustrate, homicide by an insane person and a sane person is the same physical act of man, but it is not a *human act* in both cases: the taking away of something belonging to another against the will of the owner is the same human act *materially* but not *formally* as the taking away of a thing belonging to another with the consent of the owner.

121. Lest confusion should arise in the interpretation of the thesis, a distinction must be made between *affirmative* precepts of the law and *negative* precepts. A law, in so far as it obligates to some action, is called *affirmative* or commanding; in so far as it obligates to the omission of an act, it is said to be *negative* or *prohibitive.* Moreover, commanded actions are not such that on all occasions their omission is of itself an evil, and consequently the obligation is not urged for all persons and for all times, v.g., "Honor your father and mother." On the contrary, prohibitive actions are such that they are licit for no one, for instance, "Do not steal."

Hence we have the axiom: "An affirmative law binds always, but not for always; a negative law obligates always and for always." Both laws bind *always* because there can never arise an occasion when it is licit to act against either one; but the affirmative law does not obligate *for always,* because in a change of persons or matter, the circumstances are not always present in which the law commands the action. A negative law binds *for always,* because from the nature of a prohibition the obligation is universal for all and for all time.

122. The adversaries of the thesis are: (a) Occam and his followers, who make the natural law depend upon the free will of God even after the decree of creation, and hence hold that it is extrinsically mutable by God in every case. (b) Scotus and St. Bonaventure, who taught that the natural law is dispensable in the precepts of the second table of the Decalogue. (c) Durandus, who teaches the same with regard to the affirmative precepts only of the second table of the Decalogue. The thesis has two parts:

FIRST PART

The Natural Law is intrinsically immutable

Proof

123. That law is intrinsically immutable which is a participation of the Eternal Law and which is based on rational nature in so far as it has essential relations to the end of all creation.

But the Natural Law is such a law.

Therefore, the Natural Law is intrinsically immutable.

Proof of the Major:

First, a law which is a participation of an immutable law is itself immutable. But the Eternal Law is by its concept immutable. Secondly, a law which is founded on the essences of things is immutable. But the essence of rational nature is immutable, not only in the *metaphysical* order, but even, as long as it endures, in the *physical* order.

Proof of the Minor:

Consult the theses on Eternal Law and Natural Law.

SECOND PART

The Natural Law is extrinsically immutable

Proof

124. That law is extrinsically immutable which is decreed by the will of God hypothetically necessary.

But the Natural Law is decreed by the will of God hypothetically necessary.

Therefore, the Natural Law is extrinsically immutable.

Proof of the Major:

For the will hypothetically necessary cannot be changed while the hypothesis remains.

Proof of the Minor:

Consult the theses on Eternal and Natural Law.

Scholion 1

125. With regard to the permissive Natural Law, it is to be noted that the law grants to man the right to some act with relation to his end, which act, however, is not necessary for the end. This right with regard to its exercise is subject to the social authority set up by God with relation to the end of human nature. Hence it follows: first, that since man is not obliged to exercise his right, he can omit this action according to the permission of the Natural Law; secondly, that social authority for good reason can suspend, modify or condition the exercise of this right, and in case it does the *permissive* law is not changed, but its exercise is defined within the limits of the original concession. Moreover, it is not repugnant for God to recall such a permissive right in view of a supernatural end assigned to human nature.

Scholion 2

126. For the solution of difficulties note the following:

(a) There is no parity between *positive law,* whether Divine or human, and the *Natural Law* with regard to mutability. The reason is because the positive law is *freely* decreed, while the Natural Law is *necessarily* decreed. If it is argued that the Natural Law is decreed *freely* by God, we answer that this freedom is antecedent to the decree of creation of human nature, but granted this decree, Natural Law is *necessary.*

(b) The Natural Law does not absolutely forbid homicide. It does forbid homicide by private authority and without the necessity of self-defense against an unjust aggressor. Hence in a case of legitimate self-defense, or in the execution of a just sentence of death by legitimate authority, or in the execution of God's command, as in the case of Abraham, there is no dispensation from the Natural Law.

(c) Some commentators explain the polygamy of the patriarchs on the score they acted from an erroneous conscience, influenced by the example of the infidels with whom they lived, and that they, therefore, only contracted an apparent marriage with many wives. Others hold that God changed the matter of the Natural Law with regard to polygamy. In other words, God, by a special supernatural providence, prevented the evil effects which naturally follow from polygamous marriages and which are the reasons why in Special Ethics we reject polygamy as against the Natural Law.

(d) With regard to the decrees of divorce granted to the Israelites in the Old Law, it is to be noted that in Special Ethics we reject, as against the Natural Law, divorce which is the outcome of *human* authority, whether private or public. The evils that are shown to be the result of divorce by human authority can obviously be avoided by a special providence.

TOPICS FOR DISCUSSION

1. What are the properties of the Natural Law?
2. Define "the immutability of the Natural Law."
3. What do you mean by an intrinsic change in law? By an extrinsic change?
4. How many kinds of extrinsic changes in law are there?
5. Distinguish between a formal change in law and a material change.
6. What is the difference in the nature of the command of an affirmative law and of a negative law?
7. What do you mean by saying that the Natural Law is hypothetically necessary?
8. On the fulfilment of what hypothesis does the Natural Law rely?
9. Does the restriction by positive law of a permission conceded by the Natural Law constitute a change in the Natural Law?
10. Does the killing of a man in legitimate self-defense constitute a change in the Natural Law against murder?
11. Would permission granted by God to practice polygamy or divorce constitute a material or a formal change in the Natural Law against polygamy and divorce?

THESIS XVIII

No man with developed reason can be invincibly ignorant of the primary and secondary principles of the Natural Law.

Explanation of the Thesis

127. In this thesis we discuss two other properties of the Natural Law, its *unity* and its *knowability* or *clarity*. *Unity* is present in the Natural Law because of its Author, in so far as all the precepts of the Natural Law proceed from one and the same author, God, and because of its end, in so far as all the precepts direct and order man to one and the same end. But it has another unity, which is our chief interest, viz., a unity in the order of evidence. There is one precept of the Natural Law which is *deductively* the first principle in the order of our knowledge of the Natural Law, as it is *reductively* the ultimate principle. This first principle *in the order of practical moral knowledge* is *per se* known to all men of right reason.

The necessity of a first principle in the practical order is the same as the necessity of such a principle in the speculative order. All the precepts of the Natural Law can be evident: those which are more *remotely* evident are deduced from those which are more *proximately* evident and these finally from some *one* precept more universal than all the others and containing in itself the rational basis of each precept. This is *by right* the first precept and the first principle of the Natural Law. It will be *first* not only as a precept, in so far as it does not follow any other precept, but also as a principle of knowledge, and, therefore, *in its own order* immediately or *per se* known. We say *in its own order,* i.e., in the order of *practical* moral knowledge and not in the *speculative* order. For in the *speculative* order we presuppose many things as known antecedent to the *first* moral principle, and especially the essentials of the moral order, viz., what is morally good, what is morally evil, the existence of the Eternal and Natural Law, and hence the existence and authority of the Supreme Being as Legislator. In the light of this knowledge, which is *mediate* and not *immediate* knowledge, the subject and predicate of the *first* moral principle are understood and the inclusion of the predicate in the subject is seen by inspection. In this sense, and in no other, it is asserted that the *first* moral principle, viz., the *first* principle in the moral practical order, is immediately evident or *per se* known to us. Among the principles or precepts of the Natural Law, therefore, we distinguish a *first* principle or precept, *secondary* principles or precepts and *remote* or tertiary principles or precepts.

The *first* principle of the Natural Law is that principle most universal of all, which is immediately known and from which all others are deduced. St. Thomas states it in these words: "Good must be done, evil must be avoided." This principle must be interpreted in its *composite sense,* i.e., not that everything which is good is necessarily to be done, but every good is to be done, the omission of which would be an evil and hence to be avoided. A fuller evolution of this principle reveals the following: Man is necessitated by a moral necessity arising from a law announced to him by the dictate of his reason to do that which is good and necessary for the attainment of the end of human life: by the same necessity man is obliged to avoid that which is intrinsically evil. In this fuller analysis, according to what we have seen before, this principle discloses that the human act which is necessary to produce the end of human life is commanded by a dictate of human reason, based on the Eternal Law; that the human act which frustrates the end of human life is prohibited by a like dictate of reason. Every human being, however young, as soon as he knows, either by his own effort or by the instruction of his parents or of others, the nature of moral goodness and of moral evil and that there is a Supreme Being Who governs the world, knows with *sufficiency* that good is to be done and evil is to be avoided.

Secondary principles are those which by their clear connection with the first principles are easily deduced from it. Thus, if we take the first moral principle or precept as a major premise and add a minor premise known from the natural tendencies and necessities of human life, viz., it is good for parents to love their children, we conclude to this precept of the Natural Law, "Parents are ordered to love their children."

Remote or tertiary principles are those which are derived by a more difficult process of reasoning from the first principle and the evidence for which is more remotely mediate. Such is the precept of the Natural Law against divorce.

128. By developed reason we mean, not the mere power of reasoning, but the power of reasoning developed normally and proportionately to the ordinary necessities of life according to the age of each. Just as an individual may be mentally weak and abnormal with regard to truths of the speculative order, so also he may be mentally weak and abnormal in respect to the truths of the moral practical order. Those mentally abnormal with regard to truths of the speculative or moral order are thus not included in this thesis.

It is not asserted that anyone, for any instant of time, cannot be invincibly ignorant of some one or other of the precepts included in this thesis. For invincible ignorance implies that there has been leisure proportioned to the diligent inquiry necessary for the removal of ignorance.

129. Ignorance is absence of knowledge in one who has the faculty of knowing. *Ignorance of fact* is the absence of knowledge of either the substance of a thing wished or done or of some circumstance affecting it. *Ignorance of law* is absence of knowledge of the law's existence or of the law's comprehension of this particular case. *Invincible ignorance* is absence of knowledge under such circumstances that the knowledge cannot be attained. It is *physically invincible* ignorance, if the knowledge cannot be obtained by any amount of care and diligence. It is *morally invincible* ignorance, if the knowledge cannot be attained by such an amount of care and diligence as ordinarily prudent and good men exercise under like circumstances. *Vincible ignorance* is absence of knowledge under circumstances in which knowledge can be obtained and without extraordinary effort. The question in this thesis is on ignorance with regard to the primary and secondary precepts of the Natural Law, and on *invincible ignorance* with regard to these.

Proof of the Thesis

130. If a man with developed reason, which is *per se* infallible, could be invincibly ignorant of the primary and secondary precepts of the Natural Law, the Natural Law would not be sufficiently promulgated.

But the Natural Law must be sufficiently promulgated.

Therefore, no man with developed reason, which is *per se* infallible, can be invincibly ignorant of the primary and secondary precept of the Natural Law.

Proof of the Major:

Invincible ignorance in this case would imply unavoidable and inculpable ignorance of what is necessary for the attainment of man's last end, and of what in its primary principles is self-evident, and in its secondary principles *easily* deducible from primary ones. This ignorance would be a denial that the intellect is *per se* infallible. This ignorance would arise not as a result of any deficiency in the activity of man, but as a result of a deficiency of nature in making clear, and hence *promulgating* what is necessary for the attainment of the last end, viz., the Moral Law.

Proof of the Minor:

God has ordered man to beatitude as his last natural end to be attained by actions morally good. As infinitely wise God *must* confer on man by nature what is a necessary means to this end, viz., a clear knowledge of the actions that must be done, because leading to this end, and a clear knowledge of the actions to be avoided, because leading away from this end. This is only to say that God *must sufficiently promulgate by nature* the primary and secondary principles of the Natural Law, which are in their own order self-evident with regard to primary principles and easily deducible with regard to secondary ones.

Scholion 1

131. The proof of the thesis is confirmed by the history of the human race, testifying to the existence of the "Ethical Fact." History proves that the primary and secondary principles of the Natural Law are known to all.

Scholion 2

132. No one with developed reason can be invincibly ignorant of the first principle or the first precept of the Moral Law, because such ignorance would be inculpable and hence the loss of the last end would be inculpable. In that case the loss of the last end would be due to a deficiency in nature and in the Author of Nature, and these are repugnant.

If, as a matter of fact, some men are ignorant or seem to be ignorant of the secondary principles of the Natural Law, this ignorance must be ascribed to some cause extrinsic to reason. St. Thomas assigns three such causes: (1) Bad and erroneous principles that have been induced either proximately or remotely by perverted wills; (2) corrupt habits, viz., passions developed into habits contrary to right reason; (3) evil customs, viz., practical dictates of conduct introduced by long and depraved activity. It is to be noted that ignorance of this sort, inasmuch as it is the result of a depraved will and the rejected light of reason, is *vincible,* not only in its first authors, but also in those who have erred either because of the teaching of the first authors or of the customs introduced by these. For any man, inasmuch as he has fallen from a normal condition of nature by handed-down corruption, can, by the light of reason and by the first principles of the moral order, overcome his ignorance.

Scholion 3

133. We present certain principles for the solution of difficulties urged against this thesis. Historical cases which are sometimes invoked against this thesis are: (1) Sometimes to be denied as false; (2) sometimes to be admitted as true with the comment that they manifest culpable ignorance; (3) sometimes they have reference to the more remote precepts of the Natural Law, with regard to which we admit that invincible ignorance is possible. Many historical instances, as a matter of fact, confirm our thesis. The ignorance does not fall on a secondary precept of the Natural Law but on its application in a particular case. Let us take, for instance, the practice with certain tribes of killing and eating their aged parents. The precept of honoring one's parents was known to these tribes. Their error fell on the remote precepts as to the manner in which this honor should be shown. It was thought an honor to parents to prevent their bodies from mingling with the earth and thus becoming lower than human in their composition.

TOPICS FOR DISCUSSION

1. Is the first principle of the moral and practical order antecedent to or consequent upon other principles in the speculative order?

2. What do you mean when you say that the first principle of the moral order is deductively the first and reductively the last?

3. What principle does St. Thomas assign as the first principle of the moral order?

4. Explain this principle.

5. What are secondary principles of the moral order? What are tertiary or remote principles of the moral order?

6. What do you mean by "developed reason" in the thesis?

7. Does vincible ignorance imply culpability?

8. Is vincible ignorance directly or indirectly volitional?

9. Do historical instances cited to prove man's ignorance of the secondary principles of the Natural Law actually prove their knowledge of these principles?

READINGS FOR CHAPTER VII

Adversaria Ethica, Timothy J. Brosnahan, S.J.

De Ethica Naturali, C. Macksey, S.J.

Poland, "The Natural Law," chap. iv, art. 2, p. 54; "Knowledge of the Natural Law," chap. iv, art. 5, p. 63; "Command and Prohibition," chap. iv, art. 6, p. 65; "Promulgation of the Natural Law," chap. iv, art. 3, p. 57.

Keane, part ii, "Moral Obligation and Natural Law," chap. iii, p. 101.

CHAPTER VIII

The Insufficiency of the Natural Law

THESIS XIX

For many reasons positive law must be added to Natural Law. The binding force of every positive law is ultimately based on the Natural Law. There are four essential conditions of positive law: (A) legitimate power on the part of the legislator; (B) justice; (C) possibility on the part of the matter; and (D) correct and sufficient promulgation on the part of the form.

Explanation of the Thesis

134. Positive law is a rule of action freely established by a competent authority and promulgated not in the nature of the subject, but by some external sign, oral or written. In Number 94 under Thesis XIV on the Natural Law we have already explained the essential differences between positive law and Natural Law.

135. Positive law can be based on Natural Law in two ways, either because of its *matter* or because of its *obligatory* force. Positive laws, thus based on the Natural Law, are either *declarative* or *determinative*. They are *declarative,* if they command or forbid something which by a necessary illation is deduced as necessary for good living from the principles of the Natural Law. They are *determinative,* if they command or forbid something which neither evidently nor probably can be deduced from the principles of the Natural Law. *Declarative* laws have their obligatory force from the Natural Law and are *positive* only from their mode of promulgation and the special sanction attached to them. *Determinative* laws are positive laws in the most proper sense and are derived from the Natural Law because they specify it more adequately. By reason of this specification they have binding force *immediately,* though not *ultimately,* from human power.

136. In this thesis we are considering the *ultimate* basis of the obligatory power present in positive law. This thesis is established against all those who in any way whatsoever try to derive *obligatory power* from the will of man, and *a fortiori* from *mere physical necessity.* The thesis has three parts:

FIRST PART

For many reasons positive law must be added to Natural Law

Proof

137. The Natural Law *first* is manifest to all, only with regard to its primary and secondary precepts; *secondly,* its precepts are not determined for all the variety of circumstances which obtain

in the concrete; *thirdly,* there is need of some temporal sanction for the preservation of social security. Therefore, there is need of some authority, by which, *first,* variety of opinions with regard to particular conclusions from more general principles may be prevented, and a common norm of activity for all may be established; by which, *secondly,* a practical mode of action may be determined for concrete circumstances; *thirdly,* by which temporal sanctions may be assigned for the preservation of social peace. But positive law supplies the authority for all these. Therefore, positive law must be added to Natural Law.

SECOND PART

The binding force of every positive law is ultimately based on the Natural Law.

Proof

138. Moral obligation is *final, objective* and *absolute necessity.*

But this necessity is ultimately founded on the Natural Law.

Therefore, the binding force of every positive law is ultimately based on the Natural Law.

Proof of the Major:

Consult what has been said on the nature of the obligation arising from Natural Law after the thesis on Natural Law.

Proof of the Minor:

This necessity is ultimately founded on that by which all volitional activity is *finally, objectively and absolutely necessitated.* But that by which all volitional activity is *finally, objectively and absolutely necessitated* is the Natural Law. Therefore, all moral obligation is ultimately founded on the Natural Law. Hence it follows that only the Supreme Lawgiver and he who has authority communicated from Him can impose moral obligation on the human will.

THIRD PART

139. There are four essential conditions of the positive law. And we merely state these conditions which flow as corollaries from the two parts of the thesis already established.

(a) *On the part of the legislator* is required *legitimate power* both in the matter of the law and with regard to the subjects for whom it is decreed. For the power of obligating cannot extend itself further than the communicated authority extends itself. This authority in the human legislator is restricted within limits determined both by Natural and positive law.

(b) *On the part of the matter* it is required, *in the first place,* that the law should be *just.* Moreover, the justice of the law implies two things: one with regard to the subjects, the other with regard to the end. With regard to the subjects, it is required that the law should be morally good, viz., that it be not at variance with the Natural Law or with some higher obligation of the subject. Hence human law, which is manifestly contrary to Divine law, whether Natural or positive, is invalid and no law. On the part of the end of the law it is required that it should be either necessary or useful for the common good; for the common good is of the essence of law. Hence laws which place burdens upon subjects, not for the common good, but rather to satisfy the cupidity or glory of the superior or some part of the community, are not obligatory in conscience. St. Thomas declares: "Such laws are rather violence than laws . . . hence such laws do not oblige in conscience, unless perhaps to avoid scandal or disturbance; on account of which man ought to yield his right." (S. T. 1-2, quæst. 96, art. 4.)

(c) *On the part of the matter* it is required, *in the second place,* that it should be *possible.* For no one is bound to do the impossible. A law can be said to be impossible of observance either *physically* or *morally.* It is *physically* impossible, if it absolutely exceeds the power of the subjects; it is *morally* impossible, if with respect to the power of the subjects and with respect to the proper end of the law it is extremely difficult of observance.

(d) *On the part of the form of the law* it is required that it should be correctly and sufficiently promulgated, viz., that it should be announced by legitimate authority and with widespread publicity.

Scholion

On the Cessation of Positive Law

140. A certain perpetuity or stability is of the essence of law. This perpetuity of the law can be *absolute,* viz., if by reason of the *legislator,* of the *material,* and of the *end* it is immutable. Such perpetuity cannot be ascribed to human law, since its proximate author is mutable and its matter can become deficient and the end which it seeks can cease. Thus the perpetuity of human law is only relative, that is, once decreed, it endures of itself until it is positively repealed for a just reason or automatically ceases because of changed conditions.

141. Human law can (a) *cease totally* or (b) *be repealed in part.*

(a) Human law *ceases totally:* first, by *abrogation* or *obrogation*, if, viz., the legislator positively repeals the law or decrees another law contrary to it; secondly, the law ceases totally through a cessation of its final, adequate end, viz., its intrinsic and extrinsic end. However, if there is a question of the intrinsic end there is need of a distinction; for the intrinsic end of a law can cease either *contrarily* or *negatively.* It ceases *contrarily,* if on account of a change in the matter of the law, it becomes evidently unjust to observe it; or if the object of the law becomes so hard that it is judged morally impossible with regard to the whole community; or finally if the object of the law becomes altogether useless with regard to the common good. In this case an essential condition of law is absent. The intrinsic end of a law ceases *negatively,* if in the total matter of the law there is no longer found a reason for which the law was passed, although the matter of itself is neither wrong, nor impossible, nor useless. In this case for the cessation of the law, its extrinsic end must totally cease. As an example of this, take the case of a law which imposes a tax for a certain public work; when the work is finished the law automatically ceases. *Thirdly,* the law ceases totally by a custom legitimately introduced which is contrary to the law. The legitimate introduction of a custom requires: (1) That it be good and useful for the common good; (2) that it be introduced by the community through repeated acts and with the implicit intention of imposing obligation; (3) that it be continuous, viz., prolonged through a notable length of time; (4) that the superior knows the custom and does not condemn it. The custom introduced under these conditions has the force of law and obrogates the law contrary to itself.

(b) A human law ceases partially in two ways: (1) either with regard to the matter of the law and thus we have *derogation,* which is a partial abolition of law; (2) or with regard to the subjects and so we have *dispensation,* which is a relaxation of law in particular cases by legitimate authority for a sufficient reason; or *a privilege* which is a favorable concession by the legislator to some person either physical or moral, contrary to or above the general law; or *epikeia,* which is a prudent and morally certain presumption that the law by the mind of the legislator because of circumstances not foreseen by him does not extend to this case; or *exemption,* if from the nature of the thing and the will of the legislator manifest from the beginning, an individual is excused from the law. A cessation of law which takes place through exemption or *epikeia* is not a properly so-called change of the law. Cessation of law, however, which takes place by dispensation or privilege is a change in the law because it requires an act of the legislator's will relaxing the law.

TOPICS FOR DISCUSSION

1. Define positive law.
2. What are the two ways by which positive law is based on Natural Law?
3. What do you mean by a positive declarative law? Positive determinative law?
4. What are the essential conditions for the validity of positive law?
5. What are the different ways in which positive law may cease totally? Partially?

READINGS FOR CHAPTER VIII

Adversaria Ethica, Timothy J. Brosnahan, S.J.

Rickaby, *Political and Moral Essays,* a dissertation on the Origin and Extent of Civil Authority, pp. 1-175.

Poland, "Law," chap. iv, art. 8; "Postive Law," pp. 69-75.

LeBuffe, "Other Major Divisions of Law," sect. v, pp. 49-57; "Juridical Origin of Human Positive Law," sect. vi, pp. 58-72.

Holaind, 2d lect., sect. 2 and 3, pp. 52-61.

CHAPTER IX

SUBJECTIVE PRINCIPLES OF MORALITY

THESIS XX

Conscience is the subjective norm of individual morality. Hence it is never allowed to act with an uncertain conscience. For right action, a prudentially certain conscience is sufficient, and this conscience every individual is bound to follow, even if it is invincibly erroneous. This moral certitude can be gained directly or, in a conflict of probabilities, reflexly.

Explanation of the Thesis

142. In the antecedent theses we have determined the objective norm of morality. It is now time to inquire on the application of this norm to the individual activity of the subject; for the presence of a law or a rule is not sufficient, but needs further to be applied to particular actions in the concrete. This application, however, can only be achieved through reason, which knows the general law of activity, which judges of the nature and circumstances of the act under deliberation, and which infers that this act is included or not included in a general principle of the law, and hence that there is present or not present a practical necessity of acting. This activity of reason is contained in a syllogism either expressed or tacit of which the ultimate conclusion is: *a practical judgment ultimately dictating that the action is commanded, and therefore to be performed; or prohibited and therefore to be omitted; or neither commanded nor prohibited, and therefore left to our free will to do or omit. This ultimate practical judgment is conscience, in its most proper sense.*

143. *Moral* conscience, of which there is question in the thesis, is different (a) from psychological conscience, which is intellectual knowledge of the internal affections of the subject; (b) from *intellect,* which is a potency of which moral conscience is an act; and (c) from synteresis, which is a habit of the intellect.

144. Finally in its less proper sense conscience is taken to mean the practical judgment discerning the goodness and badness of particular acts, whether they are past, actually present, or future. "Conscience is said to testify, to bind, to instigate, to accuse, to reprehend and to bring remorse. All these acts are consequent upon the application of our knowledge to the things which we do. And this application takes place in a threefold way. The first way is when we recognize that we have done something or omitted to do something . . . and according to this way conscience is said

to testify. An application is made in another way when by conscience we judge that something is to be done or not to be done, and according to this way conscience is said to *bind* or to *instigate*. An application is made in a third way when we judge by conscience that something which we have done has been done well or not, and according to this way conscience is said to *excuse* or *accuse,* or *bring remorse."* (St. Thomas, 1, quæst. 79, art. 13). Hence if the act is present or past, conscience performs the functions of judge or witness, and under this aspect it is said to testify, approve and so on. It is evident that all this is a consequence of the application of knowledge to that which we have done, and therefore that conscience, testifying, approving or excusing, is not properly a practical rule of action. We are concerned in the thesis with conscience as a proximate rule according to which an action not yet elicited, but about to be placed or omitted, ought to be directed.

145. Conscience is divided in relation to the state of mind with regard to a truth. Hence:

(a) Conscience is said to be *certain* when the mind adheres to one side of a practical contradiction without any fear with regard to the opposite. Moreover, this adherence can be *subjectively* and *objectively* certain, and then conscience is said to be *correct.* Or conscience can be only *subjectively* certain, and *objectively* false and then conscience is said to be *erroneous.* However, this error, as we indicated in the treatment of ignorance, can be either vincible or invincible.

(b) Conscience is said to be probable when for grave reasons a man adheres to one proposition, but not without fear of the truth of the opposite for which there are strong reasons. Since probability does not imply a firm adherence of the mind nor exclude all fear of the opposite, there are different degrees of probability in proportion to the importance of the motives which bring assent. Hence *probability, looked at in itself,* is said to be *strong* or *light* in accordance as the motives are capable of eliciting the assent of a prudent man or not. In comparison with the probability of the opposite proposition, probability is divided into the *highest, greater, equal, or less.* Thus one proposition with regard to another or others is said to be *most probable* or *notably more probable, equally probable* and *less probable.* The highest probability, which is called by St. Thomas *probable* certitude and by more recent writers *prudential certitude* or *broad moral certitude,* is that certitude with regard to which error is not *absolutely impossible,* although it rarely happens. The probability of the proposition opposed to *prudential* certitude is so tenuous that it can be practically neglected by the prudent in their activity. Hence we define *prudential* certitude, of which there is question in the thesis, as a *judgment made because of a reason solid enough to justify an ordinarily prudent man in acting in a matter of recognized importance.*

With regard to probability, it must be recalled from Epistemology: (a) That probability is subjective; (b) that a most probable proposition can be of itself false; (c) that in a conflict of probabilities the more probable proposition does not destroy the probability of the opposite proposition; (d) that, therefore, one can fairly assent to a less probable proposition as long as the strength of the assent does not exceed the strength of the reasons.

146. Conscience is said to be *doubtful,* if between two sides of a practical contradiction it assents to neither.

147. We, therefore, assert in the thesis that the ultimate practical dictate of conscience ought to be for right action prudentially certain. For the dictate of reason can occupy itself with the action *looked at in itself,* and then it is said to be a *remote practical dictate,* which in ethical matters is called *speculative;* or may occupy itself with an action here and now to be elicited and then it is said to be an *ultimate practical dictate.* This distinction must be clearly understood, for although the remote practical dictate may be uncertain, it is only necessary for right action that the ultimate practical dictate be prudentially certain. For this, moral certitude in its proper sense, as explained in Epistemology, is not required. Hence, because in human acts one cannot have *demonstrative* certitude, for the reason that these acts are concerned with what is contingent and variable, *prudential certitude* is sufficient. The thesis has four parts.

FIRST PART

Conscience is the subjective norm of individual morality

Proof

148. That the objective force of obligation, which is present in the Natural Law, and which through the mediation of the Natural Law is present in positive law, may exercise its efficacy in the concrete, the mere objective and indeterminate promulgation of the law is not sufficient, but it is further required that the law, to be applied individually to each and every subject in an obligatory way, should be subjectively known as a rule of action.

But the conscience of each individual performs this task.

Therefore, conscience is the subjective norm of individual morality.

Proof of the Minor:

By the constitution of nature the objective dictates of the Natural Law become known through individual reason, and by that means are applied in the concrete to individual acts. But the practical judgment of reason, by which this manifestation and application take place, is called *conscience*. Therefore, the conscience of each individual performs this task.

SECOND PART

It is never allowed to act with an uncertain conscience

Proof

149. If the dictate of conscience with regard to the obligation of law in respect to some particular action *to be elicited* or *to be omitted* is doubtful or probable, it does not exclude a prudent fear of illicit action.

But with an *actually prudent* fear that an action may be illicit it is not allowed to act.

Therefore, with an uncertain conscience it is never allowed to act.

Proof of the Minor:

The one who acts with an actually prudent fear lest the action be illicit deliberately puts himself in the danger of contracting moral evil, and with that actual disposition of the will is prepared to despise the law. But with these dispositions it is not lawful to act. Therefore, with an actually prudent fear that an action may be illicit it is not lawful to act.

THIRD PART

For right action a prudentially certain conscience is sufficient, and this conscience every individual is bound to follow, even if it is invincibly erroneous.

Proof

150. (A) For right action, that certitude is sufficient which in general the nature of the material admits; otherwise one would be bound to do that which it is impossible to do.

But in moral matters the nature of the material generally admits *only* prudential certitude.

Therefore, a prudentially certain conscience is sufficient.

Proof of the Major:

The Major is evident. For as St. Thomas says (*Com. in Eth.,* lib. 1, lect. 3): "For the disciplined man, viz., the well-instructed man, it is pertinent that he seek only that certitude in each matter which the nature of the thing allows. For he cannot have certitude with regard to variable and contingent matter as perfect as with regard to necessary matter which always exists in the same way. And so the well-disciplined man ought not to seek a greater certitude nor be content with a less certitude than that which fits in with the thing of which there is question." The Minor is clearly evident. "Because the subject-matter of prudence consists in the singular, contingent things, with which human operations are concerned, prudential certitude cannot be so perfect as to remove all solicitude." (St. Thomas, S. T. 2, 2, quæst, 47, art. 9, ad. 2.)

(B)   A prudentially certain conscience is the proximate rule of morality even if it is invincibly erroneous. The will, since it is a blind faculty, cannot be obligated otherwise than by reason or conscience by which the law is known with certitude and applied to particular cases.

But a certain conscience by its very concept is a law certainly known and applied to particular cases.

Therefore, a prudentially certain conscience is the proximate rule of morality even if it is invincibly erroneous.

Proof of the Major:

The Major is a definition.

Proof of the Minor:

It is evident that a certain conscience is clothed with the authority of the law, since it is supposed to be correct; for it is, as we have proved, the proximate norm of individual morality. It remains, therefore, to prove that part of the minor which contains the phrase, "even if it be invincibly erroneous." This is proved *negatively* and *positively*.

(a) *Negatively.* If a conscience prudentially certain, albeit invincibly erroneous, is not a norm of action, a man is bound to act contrary to that conscience or at least is allowed not to follow it. If the first is true, he is bound to act according to a law invincibly unknown to him, to attain a knowledge of which no obligation is actually present. For there cannot actually be an obligation to attain knowledge of a law, if no prudent doubt exists which would excite inquiry with regard to the existence of the law.

If the second is true, it is licit for the free will to embrace an object, which is invincibly known as an evil by an agent. Both of these suppositions, however, are obviously absurd.

(b) *Positively*. Everyone is obliged in virtue of a general principle of the Natural Law to avoid, as far as can be, evil, and for a like reason to do the good which is necessary to preserve moral order. But in virtue of this dictate, with regard to which conscience can in no sense be in error, everyone is obliged to follow conscience even if invincibly erroneous. To avoid evil and to do necessary good is dependent upon the power of man in as far as man employs moral diligence to avoid error, and in as far as the will conforms itself to that norm which according to the institution of nature is for it the proximate rule of action. With these conditions fulfilled, everyone is obliged to follow conscience and yet conscience may be invincibly erroneous.

FOURTH PART

This moral certitude can be gained directly or, in a conflict of probabilities, reflexly.

Proof

152. (A) *This moral certitude can be gained directly*. By careful investigation it is possible at times to expel all uncertainty, either with regard to a law or with regard to a fact in such wise that both the Major and the Minor of the syllogism by which the Natural Law is applied to particular cases are certain. But if these conditions are fulfilled, the conclusion or application of the law in the concrete is directly certain. Therefore, this moral certitude can be directly gained.

(B) *This moral certitude can be gained reflexly*. In a conflict of probabilities it can happen that the uncertainty concerns itself with the necessary means to a determined end, the obligation to which is absolute and efficacious; or it may be concerned with something that is licit or illicit by reason of a precept. But in both cases certitude can be gained reflexly. Therefore, this moral certitude in a conflict of probabilities can be gained reflexly.

Proof of the Minor:

(1) For as often as anyone is compelled by an absolute obligation to achieve efficaciously a determined end, he is bound to choose those means by which he will more efficaciously and

safely attain that end. The probability in this case does not follow upon the law, but on the aptitude of means to a particular end certainly intended by the law. This uncertainty can be expelled by invoking the principle, "In doubt, the safer part must be chosen; and thus is formed a conscience reflexly certain.

(2) As often as anyone, after diligent investigation, judges that an action or its omission is probably licit, he is not bound in virtue of the law to accept one side rather than the other. For the probability in this case falls on the law itself. By the invocation of the principle, "An uncertain law does not oblige," he may form a conscience reflexly certain. The reason of the principle is evident from what we have previously said with regard to the promulgation of law. For on the one side that law is not sufficiently promulgated and on the other side no end that must be efficaciously obtained from an absolute obligation is imperiled. To weaken this conclusion some ethicians invoke the other principle already cited, "In doubt, the safer part must be chosen." They hold, viz., that when there is a peril of violating the law, the safer course or that which is more favorable to the law must be chosen. To this we answer that there is no question of the election of means to an end certain and necessary, but of the intention of a particular end of an uncertain law. The law itself with regard to its present application is in doubt. The probability, therefore, falls on the particular end in the concrete, whether it is contained under the general law in the abstract. But there can be no obligation of favoring a law uncertain in the concrete.

Corollary

153. Since conscience participates in the limitations and defects of reason, it is customary to distinguish conscience by reason of the habitual state of the mind into *lax, tender, scrupulous* and *perplexed.* Conscience is said to be *lax* which rashly and for a slight reason is accustomed to judge in any matter that obligation is not present, or that malice, at least grave, is absent. Such a con-science, as is evident, is prone to confound vincible error with invincible error, and to express an opinion hardly probable as a probable opinion, or vice versa, as it favors liberty or is unfavorable to liberty. A conscience is said to be *tender* which is accustomed to inquire diligently and judge accurately of the goodness or badness of every action to be placed. A conscience is said to be *scrupulous,* which is opposed to a *lax* conscience. Thus as a *lax* conscience without sufficient reason forms a judgment in favor of liberty to avoid a law and to diminish the gravity of the

guilt, so a scrupulous conscience for the slightest reasons is accustomed to judge that an obligation is present when it is not present, and that an action is gravely wrong when it is only slightly wrong. A conscience is said to be *perplexed* which anxiously stands between two parts of a contradiction, so that it judges that it is wrong to elicit an action and at the same time that it is wrong to omit the same action.   One who labors under such a conscience according to principles already stated, ought first to suspend activity until his error or doubt is expelled; secondly, if there is present a necessity of action, he ought to do that by which he would with greater safety recede from evil, viz., he ought to choose the less evil of the two; thirdly, if he is unable to discern what is the less evil, he may choose whatever he wishes; for because of the weakness of his mind he is deficient in a necessary condition for eliciting an evil action, viz., liberty.

Scholion

Virtues as subjective co-principles of human acts

154. Principles of moral activity are either extrinsic or intrinsic.   The norm of morality and the Natural Law are extrinsic principles. The intrinsic principles are potencies, viz., the *will* and other faculties, in so far as they are subject to the command of the will, and reason or conscience, in so far as it applies the law to particular cases.   All the extrinsic principles we have sufficiently treated.   We add here a brief explanation of certain intrinsic co-principles of human acts.   For experience teaches us that we have not only *potencies* to elicit acts, but also experience sometimes *facility* or *difficulty* in producing them; and indeed in no transitory way, but *permanently*.   The principles superadded to the potencies to which this facility is ascribed are called *operative habits*.

155. A *habit* is defined as: "A quality of itself permanently superadded to a potency, by which a potency is inclined to a more ready performance of its proper acts." *Natural* habits, of which there is solely a question here, are produced through a repetition of similar acts, and once produced become in turn principles of acts, in such wise, that not only the potency in its *first* act becomes more inclined to its activity, but also its *second* act becomes easier and more perfect.

156. Our question concerns those habits by which *potencies* are perfected in the line of morals, viz., for the attaining of moral good.   These are called *moral virtues,* because in virtue of them (by the strength of them) the potencies are rendered capable of eliciting more easily acts morally good.   A moral virtue is defined as: "An operative habit perfecting rational potencies to operate according to the rule of reason." (St. Thomas 1, 2, quæst. 55, art. 1, 2, 3, 4.) For the better understanding of this it ought to be noted that "Some of the operative habits are always towards evil such as vicious habits; others sometimes towards good and sometimes towards evil, as opinion has reference to true and false," viz., the habit of opining, i.e., credulity sometimes leans to the truth and sometimes to falsehood. Virtue, however, is a habit always inclining to good. An operative habit is, therefore, evil, indifferent, or good. But human virtue, which is an operative habit, is a good habit and operative of good.

157. Virtues are divided by reason of their proper objects into those of which the immediate object is God or the last end, and into those of which the objects are the means by which the last end is attained. To the first class belong the *theological* virtues which are *Faith, Hope* and *Charity.* To the second class belong the *cardinal* virtues which are *prudence, justice, fortitude* and *temperance.* Both the theological and the cardinal virtues are generically moral virtues, for they are habits operative of good in the moral order. Nevertheless, *specifically,* the moral virtues are distinct from the theological virtues, and are exclusively called moral virtues because they do not look to the last end as their proper object, but to the means which order man to the last end.

158. The other moral virtues are reducible to the four cardinal virtues. If anyone is correctly ordered in the matter of these virtues, he will necessarily be correctly ordered in all other human operations. For the understanding of this it must be noted that we distinguish in the cardinal virtues three different kinds of parts: *integral, subjective* and *potential.* (a) The *integral* parts of a *cardinal* virtue are conditions or dispositions or functions of the soul, which, although they do not essentially constitute the habit of this virtue, nevertheless are required for the integral perfection of this virtue. (b) *Subjective* parts are complete *species* of the virtue, which, although they participate in the generic characteristic of it, nevertheless are distinct in a specific way. *Potential* parts of a virtue are certain less principal virtues which are lacking in the total potency of the principal virtue, although they are connected with it, either because they are ordered to secondary acts in the same matter, or because in other methods of procedure they are assimilated to the proper activity of the principal virtue.

159. We give a brief exposition of the moral virtues.

Prudence is defined: "The right method of things to be done." It is not to be confused with the right method of things to be made; for things to be made are constituted by external matter, but things to be done are constituted by the operating agent. Now, the right method of things to be done can be understood in a two-fold sense: one which has reference to the regulating object and that is law; the other which has reference to the potency with regard to its regulating habit, and that is *prudence.* This right method of things to be done, if looked at subjectively, is either *general* and is then called *synteresis,* or *particular,* which consists in a special application to particular activities of the principles which are stored in synteresis with regard to particular actions. Besides, the *particular* right method of things to be done can be considered as a constant and apt disposition of the practical intellect to advise rightly, judge and command with regard to things to be done; and so considered it is the *habit* of prudence. If the particular method of things to be done be considered as a judgment, by which here and now there is an actual discrimination between the conformity or non-conformity of something to be done with the law or the rule of synteresis, it is an *act of prudence.*

The things to be done, which are the object of prudence are immanent and free actions by which man acts with regard to good in its moral sense. It is to be noted, however, that although things to be done are understood first and principally as *moral entities,* those, viz., which have reference to good morals and to a moral end, nevertheless they are to be understood *secondarily* with regard to means apt and suitable to the attainment of the convenient good of human life. *Economic* prudence, v.g., has reference not only to the moral well-being of the family, but also to the well-being of the family in those things which pertain to the necessities of human life. *Political* prudence has reference not only to obedience to law, but also to the abundance of necessary things. Besides, things to be done can be considered in so far as they are the object of practical reason, or in so far as they are the object of rational or sensitive appetite. Under the first aspect they constitute the proper object of prudence as a special virtue.

160. *The parts of prudence.* (a) The potential parts of prudence are *eubulia, synesis* and *gnome.* For there are three acts with regard to things to be done; with a knowledge of the proper end to be attained by synteresis, it is necessary to take, first of all, *counsel* with regard to the means to that end, then to *judge* of their aptitude, and finally to *command,* viz., to apply all these to the action. Of these acts to *command* is the principal and pertains immediately to prudence. Three special virtues belong to counsel and judgment. *Eubulia,* or the virtue of right counsel, discovers the means that are apt to the end. Two virtues, synesis and gnome, regulate the judgment. *Synesis* regulates the judgment according to general laws; *gnome* according to higher principles. (b) The integral parts of prudence are eight, of which five have reference to prudence as an act of cognition, viz., *memory, correct valuation, reasoning, docility* and *skill;* and three, by applying knowledge to the act, have reference to prudence in so far as it is preceptive, viz., *providence, circumspection* and *caution.* (c) There are three principal subjective parts to prudence: *monastic* prudence, by which each one rules himself; *economic* prudence, by which domestic society is ruled, and *political* prudence, by which civil society is ruled.

The vices opposed to prudence through *excess* are *prudence of the flesh, cunning, guile, fraud, over-solicitude with regard to the future.* Vices that fall upon the defect of efficacy in the command of prudence are *inconstancy* and *negligence.* Vices which fall upon *defects* in counsel and in judgment are *precipitation* and *inconsideration,* of which the causes are natural *indisposition, prejudice* and *laziness.*

161. *Justice* is taken in a twofold sense for the *general* virtue and the *particular* one. Justice, taken in a general sense, is the assemblage of all the virtues which render all the operations of an agent in accordance with the law and render the agent *just.* In its general sense, justice implies *equality* with something. Since, therefore, in any act of virtue there is an equality with the rule of reason, every virtue is not without reason called a part of justice, and the collection of all *justice itself.* *Justice* as a *particular* virtue and second among the cardinal virtues is defined: "The habit according to which by a constant and perpetual will one renders to another his right."

In this definition the principal thing to be explained is "right." By the explanation of *right* it will easily be understood what is *justice,* since *right* is the proper object of justice. Now *right* can be understood in a threefold sense: (a) First, *regulatively,* for law and indeed either for every law, or for the collection of laws, or more strictly for the law determining what belongs to each one by *justice.* (b) Secondly, *fundamentally,* for the moral power founded on law, by which we vindicate something for ourselves. (c) Thirdly, *formally* as synonymous with *justice.* Although *right* taken in this threefold sense pertains to *justice,* in the first sense it is a *rule,* in the second sense it is a *presupposition,* in the third sense it is the *object* of justice. For justice establishes the equality of one person to another, which is regulated by law and based on the *moral* power of the other, and renders that to another over which he has moral power. We have treated right in the first sense or objective right in all we have said about law. We will treat of right in the second sense in the following thesis. At present there is question of right in the third sense or of the *just* thing which is the object of justice.

Although the notion of right or the just thing is sufficiently consecrated by usage, it is difficult to define what is this just thing; for as De Lugo says, "Justice is declared with relation to the just thing as its object; the just thing is declared with reference to justice, when it is said that the just thing is just." We will begin from the declaration of St. Thomas (2, 2, quæst. 57, art. 1): "It is characteristic of justice, in contradistinction to the other virtues, that it orders man in those things which have reference to another. It implies a certain equality as the name shows: for those things which are equal are said in common parlance *to be adjusted*. Equality has reference to another." Hence we derive the general difference between justice and the other cardinal virtues. Other virtues perfect man solely in those things which are a good for *himself*. But the good thing which is the object of justice is constituted by a relationship to another beside a relationship to the agent.

That which is just, therefore, implies a certain equality; this equality has reference to another through external operations, which occupy themselves with regard to means to an end. The other is a person.

162. Let us make a few statements with regard to this:

(a) First of all, the concept of that which is just is based on the objective order of things to which man has essential relationships. This order is varied according to the variety of things and relationships in which it exists. Nevertheless, all these orders are reducible to two classes: First, to the order of *operables* with regard to an end; secondly, to the order of parts of a whole in relation to each other with regard to the whole. The first order regards the *final* motions of activity, the second regards the state in which parts simultaneously existing are disposed with co-ordination to the whole. Unity is a constituent of both orders; of the first it is the common reference to one end; of the second it is the common disposition to one whole. Finally, by the unity of the first is determined the unity of the second, and the second is therefore subordinated to the first.

(b) Further, the nature of what is just, as the object of a special virtue, reposes in the order of parts to one another in relationship to the whole; not in the order of things to an end; for in this is reposed the nature of morality. This order of parts to one another in relationship to the whole is twofold: physical and moral. Just as from material entities, as parts equitably related to one another, there arises *one physical world,* so from the general association of all rational creatures, precisely as rational, there arises *one moral world,* of which the parts are persons. Both orders subsist according as the condition of right order is preserved, viz., by a consideration of different matter and of different laws, it is necessary that the parts preserve a *certain equality* to *each other* and to *the whole* or a due *quantitative proportion.* Therefore, just as in the physical world, although the things which are the parts of it are subject to perpetual changes, a physical equilibrium is preserved, and each thing is restricted by physical laws to that which is its own; so in the *moral world* there is a certain *rational equilibrium,* in which by moral laws every rational creature is restricted with regard to others taken singly and collectively.

(c) Now, this order of *quantitative proportion* of things to a whole, in so far as it has a bearing upon the moral world, is called the *order of justice.* Therefore, it is necessary that changes in this quantitative order which the number of rational agents is constantly producing, should be reduced to the formal integrity of proportion. Thus, as much as a rational creature loses of that which belongs to him, so much should be restored to him.

And so that which is just implies a certain equality of one person to another in external operations which are concerned with means to an end. From this we infer the distinction between the *objects of justice* and the *objects of the other virtues.* The object of justice is not determined by a consideration of the quality of the action of an agent. In other virtues that which is right and good is determined only according to the quality of the action of the agent.

163. The *integral* parts of justice are two, viz., to render the good that is due to another, and to avoid the evil that is harmful to another.

The subjective parts of justice are three, viz., *commutative* justice, *distributive* justice and *legal* justice. The reason of this division is explained thus: The function of justice is to set up a certain equality or a due proportion with regard to another, and, consequently, there are as many subjective parts of justice as there are relationships of one to another. But these relationships are three: (a) The relationship of part to part, or of one to another; (b) the relationship of the whole to the part, or of society to its individual members; (c) the relationship of part to the whole or of individual members to society.

Accordingly, (1) *commutative* justice refers to the relationship of one individual to another; and regards the equality of thing to thing, as they say the *arithmetic* equality, nor does it regard the quality of the person except accidentally, in so far as for this reason the thing itself is differentiated. The object of this justice is *mine* and *thine*. It belongs to the dignity of a rational being, as perfectly subsisting in itself, that, first, by nature it is not a mere means ordered for the utility of another, and, secondly, that other things are ordered to the utility of itself. Some of these other things are common, as air and light, in the use of which no preference is given to one over another. There are certain other things, however, which because of the nature of the things, or of some contingent fact, have a particular connection with one person so that the total utility of them ought to be referred to him. Hence the just thing which is called *mine* and *thine* and which commutative justice aims to safeguard includes all these latter things.

(2) *Distributive* justice has reference to the community or him who has care of the community, with regard to the inferior, and it regards not an equality of thing to thing, but the proportion between the merit and dignity of one and the merit and dignity of another. Thus it is said to observe *geometric* proportion. The subject of this virtue is the superior of the community, who is bound to distribute common advantages and duties according to the merit and quality of each one.

Some divide distributive justice into *remunerative* and *vindicative* justice according as it distributes rewards or punishments. Others disagree, because sometimes in the distribution of rewards or punishments other species of justice intervene.

(3) *Legal* justice refers to subjects in relation to the community, and regards the proportion to be observed between the activity of the subjects and the common good of society. This virtue particularly sees to it that the laws are observed and preserved in their force, in so far as by the observance of law the common good is promoted. And so legal justice is not to be confused with obedience or with piety towards one country, for: (a) *obedience* inclines *formally* to the rectitude of due observance and subjection to superiors, whilst legal justice looks on the rectitude of obedience in order to the common good; (b) piety inclines to reverence for one's country, because we are born in it or because we are maintained by it, but it does not regard the common good of the society as such. Hence legal justice is specifically the same in the superior and in the subject, because in both it regards the same formal object, viz., the common good.

Legal justice is sometimes called general by reason of the command which it places on other virtues that can be directed to this object. Nevertheless, it is not to be confused with general justice considered as a collection of all virtues; for legal justice has its own proper object.

164. The *potential parts* of justice in relation to *God* are *religion, obedience* and *penance;* in relation to parents, relatives and country, *piety;* in relation to superiors of whatever kind, *observance;* in reference to all others, *love, affability* and *truth;* in reference to certain others, for a special reason, *liberality, fidelity, gratitude* and *vindication.*

165. *Fortitude* is the virtue which restrains fear and moderates boldness in the presence of perils that make it difficult for the soul to restrict itself to the rules of reason. Thus, it orders the *irascible* passions. The *remote* object of fortitude, or that about which it operates, is serious danger, especially that of death. The *proximate* object is twofold: internal and external. The *internal* object is the interior motions of fear and boldness, which arise in the irascible appetite in the presence of danger. The *external* object is exterior actions, as aggression and flight. The *formal* object is the special rectitude which is evident in this, that we bear, or attack, according to the rule of reason, dangers which are apprehended under the aspect of what is *arduous.*

The parts of fortitude are four, viz., *magnanimity, magnificence, patience* and *perseverance.* There are two acts of this virtue: to *attack* and to *sustain.* From the standpoint of *aggression,* a brave heart is requisite in defence of good which belongs to *magnanimity,* and further it is requisite that the soul should not be deficient in the execution of its projects, which belongs to *magnificence.* From the standpoint of *endurance,* it is requisite that the will be not broken by evil circumstances and this is the function of *patience;* that it be not fatigued by the persistence of evil and this is the function of *perseverance.* Under patience we can include *longanimity,* by which the soul awaits for a long time without despair the deferred good; and *constancy,* by which the soul sustains the labors arising from a sustained execution of a good work.

The *vices* which in general are opposed to fortitude are: *timidity,* which is excessive fear of danger; *cowardice,* which is a defect contrary to aggression; *fearlessness,* which is a deficiency in fear; and *rashness,* which is an excess in aggression. In particular, *pusillanimity* by defect and *presumption* by excess are opposed to magnanimity. *Parsimony* by defect and *extravagance* by excess are opposed to magnificence. *Impatience* by defect and *stubbornness* by excess are opposed to perseverance.

166. *Temperance* is the virtue which moderates the sensitive appetites with regard to pleasure, because of the special goodness which is apparent in such moderation. It, therefore, regulates the *concupiscible* passions. The *remote* object of temperance is things the use of which brings sensible pleasure; the *proximate* object is these pleasures.

The *subjective parts of temperance* are four: *abstinence* and *sobriety,* which moderate appetites that have reference to the conservation of the individual; *chastity* and *modesty,* which moderate appetites bearing on the conservation of the species.

The *potential parts of temperance* are four: *Continence,* which restrains the will from following the impulse of passion; *meekness,* by which the passion of anger is controlled; *clemency,* by which just punishment is mitigated, and *moderation,* by which one contents himself within the limits of his state, his talents and the condition of his life. Connected with moderation are: *humility,* by which the tendency to undue self-exaltation is controlled; *philotimia,* by which one seeks according to necessity ordinary and fitting honor; *studiousness,* by which one strives for the knowledge becoming his state of life; *restrained manners,* by which one conducts himself correctly in serious external activity; *eutrapalia,* by which one carries himself congruously in recreations and games; *moderate adornment,* which concerns itself with the proper external appearance.

167. What is the meaning of the saying: "Virtue stands in the middle"?

"The good of anything," says St. Thomas (1, 2, quæst. 64, art. 3), "stands in the middle, according as it is conformed to rule or measure, when there is a chance of transcending or being deficient with regard to the rule or measure." Therefore, since virtue has a relation to right reason, as the thing measured to the measure, its good consists in conformity to its rule. Its evil flows from the fact that it either exceeds the measure or is deficient with regard to it. Hence virtue is said to consist in a certain mediation between extremes which are excess and defect.

The mean is found in virtues either *per se* or *per accidens; per se,* if the matter of the virtue allows a mean; *per accidens,* if the matter of the virtue does not admit a mean, but excess or defect can arise from the agent. Hence:

(a) In the theological virtues *per se* there is no mean. The rule of faith is Divine truth; of hope, Divine omnipotence and piety; of charity, Divine goodness. To believe in God, to hope in God and to love God, as is right, do not admit any mean. *Per accidens,* these do admit a mean from our part, because we ought to tend towards God according to our measure. Thus, one who hopes from God a good which exceeds his condition is said to *presume,* and one who does not hope according to his condition is said to despair.

(b) In the *moral* virtues *per se* there is a mean. This is twofold, viz., a mean of *reason* and of *thing.* The *mean of reason* is that measure of activity which, with attention to the circumstances of the agents, of place, of time and other like, is conformable to right reason, and this mean can be different with differentiation of agents. The *mean of thing is* that measure which arises from the thing materially considered with which the action concerns itself. It is not, therefore, variable as the mean of reason, but from the nature of the case is invariable. Hence prudence looks to the *mean of reason,* in so far as it assigns to the other virtues by its command this *mean;* and hence by understanding and commanding this measure it apprehends its own mean. *Fortitude* and *temperance* preserve the mean of reason, in so far as they moderate the passions according to right reason. *Justice* ought to preserve both the mean of thing and the mean of reason: the mean of thing since the matter of justice is a debt to be rendered according to equality; the mean of reason, since, in order that an act of justice be formally virtuous, prudence must determine whether under the circumstances the debt is to be paid or denied.

TOPICS FOR DISCUSSION

1. Define moral conscience in its most proper sense.
2. How is moral conscience distinct from psychological conscience and from synteresis?
3. Does moral conscience in its most proper sense deal with past acts?
4. Define certain conscience; erroneous conscience.
5. Define probable conscience and prudential certitude.
6. If the doubt of our conscience falls on a law or the application of a law to a particular case and no certain rights of others are jeopardized, on what basis may we apply the principle, "A doubtful law does not oblige"?

READINGS FOR CHAPTER IX

Adversaria Ethica, Timothy J. Brosnahan, S.J.

Catholic Encyclopedia, "Conscience," vol. iv, p. 268; "Virtue," vol. xv, p. 472; "Vice," vol. xv, p. 403; "Cardinal Virtues," vol. iii, p. 433; "Prudence," vol. xii, p. 517; "Justice," vol. viii, p. 571; "Fortitude," vol. vi, p. 147; "Temperance," vol. xiv, p. 481.

Glenn, "Conscience," chap. iii, p. 83.

Poland, chap. v, "Moral Conscience," pp. 75-81; chap. vi, "Aids and Hindrances to Observance of Moral Order," pp. 86-90.

Leibell, "The Cardinal Virtues," p. 236; "Synteresis," p. 341; "Conscience," pp. 344-355.

Cronin, "Of Synteresis," chap. xvi, pp. 537-572; "The Moral Faculty," chap. xiv, pp. 472-505; "Of Habits and Virtues," chap. xviii, pp. 593-632.

Holaind, "Justice," 6th lect., pp. 151-171.

Keane, part i, "Moral Virtue," chap. vi, p. 66.

Rickaby, *Moral Philosophy*, "Of Habits and Virtues," chap. v, pp. 64-109; "Of the Natural Law of Conscience," chap. viii, pp. 133-159.

CHAPTER X

RIGHTS AND DUTIES

Introduction

168. In preceding chapters we have explained and demonstrated the goal towards which man ought to tend by his volitional activity. We likewise established the moral necessity by which man is impelled towards this goal, and the conditions with which his actions ought to be clothed in order that he may be right and good in relationship to this goal. Certainly the *duty* imposed on man by moral obligation implies the *right* of *immunity* from undue interference by others in the fulfilment of duty. Hence before we proceed to apply the basic principles of Ethics to the various kinds of human activity, viz., man's volitional activity in relation to God, to himself and to his fellowman, it is necessary to establish true principles with regard to rights and duties.

With regard to rights and duties in general, we will consider: first, what is right, and what are its elements; secondly, what is duty; thirdly, what is the basis of rights and duties; fourthly, what are the attributes of right, viz., limitation, collision and coercion.

THESIS XXI

Right is correctly defined: the moral and inviolable power of possessing, of doing, or of exacting something. The subject and term of right are necessarily intelligent beings. The title of right is some contingent fact by which right is actuated in the individual. The matter of a right can never be a person.

Explanation of the Thesis

169. (1) Right is understood in a threefold sense:

(a) First, *regulatively,* for the law and indeed either for every law, or for the collection of laws, or more strictly for the law determining what belongs to each one by *justice.*

(b) Secondly, *fundamentally* or *subjectively,* as it were, for the moral power founded on law by which we vindicate something for ourselves.

(c) Thirdly, *formally,* as synonymous with the *just.* Although right considered in these three ways belongs to *justice,* nevertheless, in the first way it is a *rule,* in the second way it is a *presupposition,* in the third way it is the *object of justice*. For justice, as we said previously, brings about an *equality* of one to another, which is regulated by *law* and based on the moral power of another and delivers that to which another has moral power. We considered right taken in the first sense in the whole treatise on Natural Law; we treated right in the third sense in the last thesis under the moral virtue of justice; in this thesis we are treating of right as the moral power by which we vindicate something for ourselves, or the moral power which each one has with regard to those things which are *his own* or with regard to those things which are due to him. In this sense right differs from right considered as *law* or as synonymous with what is *just;* first, because law and what is just connote objective obligation by which human liberty is restricted; but moral power asserts moral liberty and thus connotes negation of obligation; secondly, law and what is just are primarily objective, whilst moral power is primarily something subjective although founded on the objective order and connoting something objective.

(2) *Subjective* right is defined: The moral and inviolable power of possessing, doing or exacting something. It is said to be:

(a) A *power,* because it implies a certain capacity in virtue of which a person *can* (possess, do or exact) and so is different from *duty* which is the relationship in virtue of which a person *owes* something.

(b) *Moral,* because it is not exercised by physical influence, but is a power conceded by some law, to be acknowledged by others, which exercises its influence by means of reason on the free will of another.

(c) Of *possessing, doing or exacting something,* because the matters with which this power is concerned are *things,* or *personal activity,* or the *activity of others.* By the term *things* we understand *extrinsic things,* and goods *intrinsic* both to body and to soul. By the term *activities* we understand both actions and omissions.

(d) *Inviolable,* because it binds free wills with regard to the *matter* of a right; *negatively,* lest these free wills should interfere with the one possessing a right in its *exercise; positively,* that these free wills should render that which is exacted of them in virtue of a *right.*

Hence (1) right implies two things: *liberty* on the part of the subject of the right, and obligation on the part of others to reverence this right. (2) Right is different, first of all, from negative liberty or from the simple power of doing something; such a power is indeed *moral,* but there is no strict obligation on the part of others to acknowledge and reverence it. In the second place, right is different from a certain rational convenience in doing something, because this rational convenience implies no strict obligation on the part of others. In the third place, right is different from that right which is called *precarious,* viz., from a concession granted, but revocable. There is no reason, however, why a precarious right should not be clothed with the characteristics of true right with regard to others, who can neither grant nor recall the right.

(3) Since right consists in a certain relation, we can distinguish in it, as in other relations, *subject, foundation* and *term.* The *subject* of a right is any individual who is vested with a right, whether such is a physical or a moral personality. The *foundation* of a right is either that on which the right is *ultimately* based, viz., the *principle* of a right; or that by which the right is proximately actuated, viz., some contingent fact in virtue of which the right is proximately determined in an individual. This latter is called the *title* of a right. The *term* of a right is either that over which or in regard to which a person is said to have a right, and this is properly called the *matter* of the right, viz., something possessed or to be done or to be exacted; or it is a person in whom is found the duty corresponding to the right. Such a person is properly called the *term* of the right and like the subject of right can be either a physical or a moral personality. In the present thesis there is question of the subject, title, matter and term of rights. The thesis has four parts.

FIRST PART

Right is defined: The moral and inviolable power of possessing, of doing, or of exacting something.

Proof

170. Right by an analysis of its concept connotes the relationship of man to man in the order of justice to be preserved.

But such a relationship is the moral and inviolable power of possessing, of doing, or of exacting something.

Therefore, right is defined: the moral and inviolable power of possessing, of doing, or of exacting something.

Proof of the Major:

The Major is evident from what has already been said about justice in Nos. 162 and 163.

Proof of the Minor:

The relationship of man to man in the order of justice to be preserved necessarily implies the moral power of preserving or restoring the equilibrium of the moral world, by which man can possess what is his own, legitimately exercise his own activity, and exact from others what is due to him. Since this order of justice is a part of the moral order, this moral power demands acknowledgment and reverence and is consequently inviolable.

SECOND PART

The subject and the term of right are necessarily intelligent beings.

Proof

171. The subject of a right is one possessed of a moral power; the term of a right is one who has an obligation to respect the moral power of another.

But those possessed of moral power and those who have an obligation to respect the moral power of another are necessarily persons.

Therefore, the subject and the term of right are necessarily intelligent beings.

Hence it follows: First, that the *right itself* is one thing, the exercise of right is *another thing*. For an intellectual being, before he arrives at the use of reason, can have a right with regard to many things without, however, having the power to exercise his right. And so it follows that for a person to be the subject of a right the use of reason is not required. Secondly, the subject of a right must be in actual existence, but not the term of the right. The reason of the first is because a power without a subject in which it inheres is not a power. Nevertheless, it can happen that an action now elicited can injure a future man, if the action remains in its effect until the man be born. The reason of the second is because it can happen that a person be vested with a right by which not only living men are bound, but also other men as soon as they exist.

Moreover, it follows from the proof of this part that brute animals cannot have rights and consequently men cannot have duties towards them, although they may have duties with regard to them, as they have with regard to all other created things which are subjected to their service. Wherefore, to inflict pain on animals when such pain has reference to the utility of man is licit. But to torture animals without a reasonable cause is illicit, because such torture in general debases the soul of the torturer, renders it insensible with regard to suffering and inclines it to cruelty. Besides, it is an injury to the Creator irrationally to abuse the gifts constituted by His bounty.

THIRD PART

The title of right is some contingent fact by which right is actuated in the individual.

Proof

172. The title of right is the objective reason from which arises proximately in the concrete a definite inviolable moral power by which a certain moral preference is conferred on one person, and in virtue of which he is preferred to all others in the *possession* of a thing, or in an *action* to be *placed,* or in a *thing* or an *action* to be *exacted.*

But this objective reason is some contingent fact by which the right is actuated.

Therefore, the title of right is some contingent fact by which right is actuated in the individual.

Proof of the Minor:

This objective reason is either the very existence of a nature, by reason of which, from a right of nature prohibiting injury, there belongs to an existent rational nature the right lest it should be harmed by others in the good granted to it as its own by God; or is some fact which is added to nature already constituted in existence, and, therefore, a contingent fact, by reason of which from a precept of Natural Law a competency is granted to the rational creature that his own should be conferred on him by others. Therefore, the objective reason is some contingent fact by which the right is actuated.

FOURTH PART

The matter of a right cannot be a person

Proof

173. In order that something be the object of human power it is necessary that it should be by its nature subjected to man, as a rational entity.

But a rational being, because it is of its own right and a person, cannot be by nature subordinated to another person.

Therefore, the matter of right cannot be a person.

Proof of the Major:

The Major is evident.

Proof of the Minor:

The Minor is developed by a solution of the difficulties which might seem to invalidate the conclusion. First of all, it is argued that the superior has a right over his subjects and the father a right over his children. To this it is answered that such a right is the right of governance by which the actions of the subject or of children are directed for their utility or for the common good; that such a right by no means implies a competency in the superior or the father of using subjects or children, as if they were mere means for the utility of the superior or the father. Secondly, it is argued that the master has a right over servants, to direct them in their activity for the utility of the master. To this it is answered that the master has no right over the person of the servants, but over their activities. For the servant has of his own right certain connatural rights which the master is obliged to acknowledge and reverence. Therefore, it is one thing to have a right over a person and another thing to have a right over some action of that person, over his work or his service. Absolute servitude by which one man would be subject to another as a thing can never be juridically legitimate.

TOPICS FOR DISCUSSION

1. What are the three different ways in which right may be considered?
2. Define subjective right.
3. How does a moral power act?
4. If subjective rights are inviolable, how does it happen that they are violated?
5. What two things are implied in a subjective right?
6. Distinguish between the subject, the foundation and the term of a right.
7. How is the title of a right distinguished from the ultimate basis of a right?
8. Have brute animals rights?
9. Can infants in the womb have rights?

THESIS XXII

A juridical duty is a moral debt to do or to omit something in favor or help of another by reason of commutative justice. Not all the duties of the Natural Law are juridical. To every duty there corresponds a right in the subject, consequent upon an obligation inherent in him. To a juridical duty in one person corresponds a right in another, and this right is the basis of the duty.

Explanation of the Thesis

174. Duty, abstractly considered, is said in general to be any obligation because of which a person in virtue of the rational order is bound to an action or an omission. *Duty,* considered in the *concrete,* is in general the action or omission to which the obligation has reference. Besides, in the popular sense, duty is usurped to designate a social function in virtue of which special duties are incumbent upon him who is the subject of the social function. It is common to all duties, taken in the generic signification, that they are founded, either mediately or immediately on the objective rational order and consequently on the Natural Law, just as all moral obligation. In this sense all duties are *ethical.* The concept of moral obligation and the concept of duty are, however, distinct, because, in the first place, in *moral obligation* the order between *subject* and *superior* is considered, but in *duty* the order between *equals* is considered. In the second place, *obligation* is an ordination for the good of the subject, but duty is an ordination for the good of another, which, therefore, is obligation in reference to the *social order.*

175. Duties are distinguished into those which are *merely ethical* and those which are besides *juridical.* A *juridical* duty is that which corresponds to a *perfect right,* a right, viz., in the strictest sense of the word. A *perfect right* is that which is the object of commutative justice, and, according to some, of legal justice. This right, therefore, implies, in the first place, that the thing with which the right is concerned is connected with us in such a special way that its total utility is in our power to the exclusion of others. In the second place, a perfect right implies such an inviolability that we have the power to seek and exact the things that belong to us. In the third place, a perfect right implies that we can legitimately defend the inviolability of our right with coercion. An *imperfect right* is a right not vested with these characteristics. Such rights are those which arise from distributive justice and from the potential parts of justice or from those virtues which are connected with justice.

The correlative of a *perfect right* is *juridical duty*. It is distinguished from *moral obligation as such* and from a *merely ethical duty*, first, because its violation inflicts an *injury* on the subject of the right. And so it is necessary to distinguish between *injury* and *offense*. For an offense is that by which one is made rationally opposed to us, which can happen without the violation of a perfect right. A perfect right is different, secondly, from a merely ethical duty because by the violation of a juridical duty one is bound to restitution.

The Thesis has four parts.

FIRST PART

A juridical duty is a moral debt to do or to omit something in favor or help of another by reason of commutative justice.

Proof

176. A juridical duty is a moral obligation corresponding to a perfect right.

But a moral obligation corresponding to a perfect right is a moral duty to do or omit something in favor or help of another by reason of commutative justice.

Therefore, a juridical duty is a moral debt to do or omit something in favor or help of another by reason of commutative justice.

Proof of the Major:

The Major is a definition. Confer Nos. 174 and 175.

Proof of the Minor:

For no inviolable moral power or right can exist or be conceived, to which there does not correspond in others the moral obligation of doing or omitting all those things which are necessary, lest the possessor of the right according to its basis, in this case commutative justice, should have his power in vain.

SECOND PART

Not all the duties of the Natural Law are juridical

Proof

177. The duties of the Natural Law are divided into duties towards God, towards ourselves and towards others, and have reference to internal and external acts, and merely personal and social acts.

But many of these acts are not acts of commutative justice.

Therefore, not all the duties of the Natural Law are juridical.

Proof of the Major:

Duties are divided according to the terms towards which the acts are formally directed. But these terms are no other than God, ourselves and others. For we have no duties towards beings without reason, since they cannot be the subjects of right.

Proof of the Minor:

(a) Duties towards God, as indeed all duties also towards ourselves and others, are, in relation to God, juridical; since through any violation of these injury is inflicted on the external glory of God. But with regard to other men, duties towards God cannot be called juridical; for others have not the perfect right that they should be fulfilled, nor is injury inflicted on others by the violation of them. (b) Duties towards ourselves, as is manifest, are not exacted by commutative justice. (c) Many duties towards others are exacted by distributive justice, by charity, by gratitude, or by other virtues connected with justice, which can be omitted without injury to others. Many duties besides are fulfilled or violated by internal acts.

THIRD PART

To every duty there corresponds a right in the subject, consequent upon an obligation inherent in him.

Proof

178. Every duty, whether it be merely ethical or juridical, implies a moral obligation, founded on the Natural Law, either immediately or mediately, and for that reason binds the free will.

But the subject of a duty, who is bound by law to its fulfilment, by that very fact, has from the same law the inviolable moral power of fulfilling that duty.

Therefore, to every duty there corresponds a right in the subject, consequent upon an obligation inherent in him.

Proof of the Major:

The Major is a definition.

Proof of the Minor:

Whenever a moral obligation is imposed by law upon someone, there is necessarily conceded to him at the same time a moral power which others are bound to acknowledge and reverence. For an obligation, the fulfilment of which others could legitimately impede, implies that one and the same law concedes the power of acting contrary to that which it commands. Therefore, one who has an obligation has the right of fulfilling his obligation.

FOURTH PART

To a juridical duty in one person corresponds a right in another, and this right is the basis of the duty.

Proof

179. A juridical duty is a duty towards another, which cannot be omitted without injury.

But to such a duty there corresponds a right in another, which is the basis of the duty.

Therefore, to a juridical duty in one person corresponds a right in another, and this right is the basis of the duty.

The Major and Minor are both evident.

Scholion

180. The equality which is safeguarded by commutative justice is twofold: (a) The equality, which is considered in the things which justice commands to be rendered; (b) the equality which is considered in the persons between whom there exists a juridical relation. The first equality is real; the second is personal. Now, just as in the equilibrium of the physical world, it is not required that all things should be vested with the same activities, but that each thing should have its own proper activity, so, in the moral world, it is not necessary for real equality that all should have the same things, but that each one should possess his own things. In the same way, personal equality does not consist in the fact that all men have exactly the same rights, but in a certain mutual independence, in virtue of which each one belongs to himself and not to another. That all men are equal is indubitable, if we look at the common nature and the ultimate end of each individual, and if we look at the rights and duties which flow from these. But since the talents of all cannot be equal, and each individual differs from another in qualities of soul and body, there are many dissimilarities in character, will and nature. And so nothing can be so repugnant to nature as to wish to embrace in one category all things, and to reduce all things to this category by civil institutions.

Wherefore, if one belongs to another under certain formalities, in this respect there cannot be equality, and consequently right in its simple sense. But as we proved in the preceding thesis, one cannot simply belong to another, so that he is in no sense of his own right. The son, in so far as he is the son, belongs to the father, and likewise, the servant, in so far as he is the servant, belongs to the master; both, however, if we consider them as individual men, are subsistent in themselves and distinct from others. And therefore, in so far as both are men, there is a relation of justice with regard to them.

The basis, therefore, of equality or of mutual independence among men, is that element in which all men are alike, viz., rational nature and the dignity of human nature by reason of its subordination to the First Cause and its destiny with regard to the Last End.

TOPICS FOR DISCUSSION

1. Define duty.
2. Distinguish between merely ethical duties and juridical duties.
3. What is the difference between the concept of moral obligation and the concept of duty?

THESIS XXIII

The juridical order is contained within the moral order as a constituent part. Therefore, those theories must be rejected which derive the origin of right from force or from physical necessity, or solely from personal liberty looked at in itself.

Explanation of the Thesis

181. The juridical order is the hierarchical assemblage of juridical laws, of perfect rights and of juridical duties. We assert that this order belongs to the moral order, as an external part of it, in so far as it regards external acts of the social life. We do not assert that all rights, duties and laws of the juridical order belong to the moral order with the same immediacy.

182. *Division of rights.* Rights are *natural* or *positive,* in accordance as they are an *immediate* concession of the Natural Law or a *mediate* concession through the human will, whether that is brought about by a private contract or by positive law. Moreover, in accordance with the diversity of positive law, a right can be conceded by Divine or human positive law. These human laws may be either civil or ecclesiastical, written or traditional. It must be noted that certain rights, which seem to be derived from positive law, are in reality from the Natural Law which is *declared* by positive law.

Rights are *connatural* or *acquired,* according as their title is the fact of existence, or some other fact, whether necessary or free, which is consequent upon existence.

Rights are *inalienable* or *alienable*. An inalienable right is one than can neither licitly nor validly be abdicated by man, because it is a necessary condition of attaining the last end or of fulfilling a determinate moral obligation.

Rights are *jurisdictional* or *proprietary* in a broad sense. A *jurisdictional* right is the right of governing subjects and of directing them for the common good. A *proprietary* right is the power to dispose of the matter of a right for one's own convenience. *Proprietary* rights are *over the thing* or *with regard to the thing,* according as one has immediately in his possession the thing, which is the matter of the right, or does not immediately possess this thing, but has the right that it should be yielded to him. *Proprietary* right is also divided into *personal* and *real* right, according as the right immediately inheres in a person, or is connected with a thing, and through the mediation of a thing, belongs to the person who has a right over that thing.

183. Duties are divided into *natural* and *positive;* into *affirmative* and *negative;* into *connatural* and *adventitious;* into *merely ethical* and *juridical;* into duties *towards God, towards ourselves,* and *towards others.* These divisions are clear from what has already been said.

184. All false opinions on the basis of the juridical order are ultimately reducible to two classes: (a) The class of those who derive ultimately the origin of right from physical force; (b) the class of those who derive it in some way from the free will of man.

(a) Hobbes, who in substance is followed by all of those who constitute utility as the norm of morality, revived the doctrines of the first class. I say *substantially* or *objectively* and with regard to fundamental principles. For, logically from the principles of these philosophers, it follows that every right is ultimately based on physical force. It is of no moment that these philosophers hold ideas about justice, benevolence and liberty, which *in appearance* seem to imply the basis of right which we have laid down. This only proves that, either they intend to bewilder the minds of their readers or that their own minds are bewildered. They hold, therefore, in the first place, that outside of society in a "state of nature," all men have rights to all things, provided they are able to pursue those rights; for *right* and *useful* signify the same thing. Hobbes says in his *Rudimentary Philosophy concerning Government and Society,* Chap. 1, No. 14: "From whence we may understand likewise as a corollary, in the natural state of man, that a *sure and irresistible power confers the right of dominion and ruling over those who cannot resist; in so much as the right of all things that can be done adheres essentially and immediately unto this*

omnipotence thence arising." In the second place, these philosophers hold that this state of nature cannot endure, since it carries
with it the warfare of all against all; and so civil society is necessary; and that civil society is the source of all rights, in so far
as it is the receptacle of the rights received from all, which after-
wards it distributes for peace and the common good.

The opinion which Spencer proposed derives the juridical order
from evolutionary physical necessity. Although he often speaks
of liberty, the term cannot be taken in its proper sense in his
works, for he denied entirely the free will of man which is the
basis of all external active liberty.

To this class must be added those jurists of our time, whose
doctrine is contained in these formulas: "Right consists in a
material fact; and human duties are an empty name, and all human
facts have the force of right"; "The unjust fact of happy issue, in
no wise prejudices the sanctity of the right (thence arising)";
"The civil state, being the source and fountain of all rights, possesses a right which knows no limits." (These three propositions
are propositions 59, 61, 39, contained in the Syllabus or a collection of errors condemned by Pius IX, December 8, 1864. Cf.
Wilmer's Handbook of the Christian Religion, Appendix 3.)

(b) Kant made a distinction between the ethical and juridical
order and affirmed them to be mutually independent. The ethical
order has reference to internal acts, or external acts, placed from
the ultimate internal motive of morality. The juridical order has
reference to external acts, placed from external motives. The end
of the ethical order is to procure internal liberty; the end of the
juridical order to procure external liberty. *Internal liberty* consists in the independence of the will from every empirical motive
and from external coercion, and hence in the *autonomy* of the
will. *External liberty* has reference to external and social acts
and its necessary condition is coercive legislation, by which alone
external liberty can exist between co-existing persons, and by
which the liberty of individuals ought to be coerced in favor of the
liberty of all. Hence all external legislation, even Divine, implies
heteronomy of the will.

Hence it follows that the actions, which autonomous reason
(autonomous reason in the mind of Kant is the will) categorically
commands, are *ethical;* and actions, which a law extrinsic to autonomous reason commands, are *juridical,* and so subject to coercion.
As Kant says: "It is not an ethical duty to keep one's promise, but
a legal duty, one that we can be compelled to perform." Right,
therefore, and the power of coercion, are the same thing. The
power of coercion arises from the necessity of reconciling the per-

sonal liberty of one with the personal liberty of all. Since *right* has no admixture of the ethical, the basis of it is derived solely from the personal liberty of each and of all.

Hence, in Kant's opinion the *juridical order* is the assemblage of the conditions under which the free will of one can harmoniously coexist with the free will of another according to the universal law of liberty.

The thesis has three parts.

FIRST PART

The juridical order is contained within the moral order as a constituent part.

Proof

185. The juridical order is the assemblage of juridical laws, juridical duties and perfect rights.

But these three (a) are subject to the moral order; (b) as constituent parts of it; (c) and, indeed, external parts.

Therefore, the juridical order is contained within the moral order as a constituent part.

Proof of the Major:

The Major is a definition.

Proof of the Minor:

(a) In the first place we have already proved that all laws are either the Natural Law, or at least laws declarative or determinative of the Natural Law, which ultimately derive their obligatory force from the Natural Law. Therefore, juridical laws have their binding power from one and the same source. In the second place, juridical duties are either natural or positive. Both of these are contained within the moral order, for they are duties just in proportion as they impose moral obligation. All moral obligation, however, as finally based on the Natural Law, is contained within the objective moral order. In the third place, right is perfect to the extent that there corresponds to it a juridical duty; each, therefore, by an internal and necessary correlation mutually demands the other, since in this correlation the peculiar inviolability of right consists. Therefore, there is the same origin for each of the correlates. Since every duty either mediately or immediately is a consequence of Natural Law, every perfect right is contained within the moral order.

(b) The juridical order has the same relation to the moral order, as what is just has to what is good. But what is just is a constituent part of goodness in the line of morals. And so the juridical order is a constituent part of the moral order.

(c) The juridical order looks to the external acts of the social life. But not the whole social life belongs to the juridical order, since there are many duties pertaining to the social life which are not juridical. But it is manifest that social operations are related to the whole moral life of man, as an external part to the whole, which is made up of internal and external elements. Therefore, the juridical order contains external social acts of the moral order.

Corollary

186. As positive law is a necessary complement of the Natural Law, so the positive juridical order is a necessary complement of the natural juridical order. First of all, the natural juridical order embraces many indeterminate, imperfect and doubtful rights and duties of social and civil life, which must be made determinate, perfect and certain for the stability of social and political life. In the second place, every perfect right is inviolable; nevertheless, that this inviolability may be efficaciously preserved and safe-guarded, there is need of the protection of positive law. In the third place, the power of coercion, which is necessarily connected with the inviolability of a perfect right, cannot be exercised indiscriminately by every citizen, because this would invite disorder in socal life. Hence it is necessary for positive law to determine the *manner* and *measure* of this coercion, and it should declare, that, in most cases, the coercive right is to be exercised by those alone who have authority in the community.

SECOND PART

Therefore, those theories must be rejected which derive the origin of right from force or from physical necessity.

Proof

187. The juridical order, as the order of justice, is related to the moral order as an external and constituent part.

But it is absurd to derive the principle of any part of the moral order from prevalent physical might, whether of an individual or of many united in society, whether this power is identified with the power of the strong or with mere physical necessity.

Therefore, those theories must be rejected which derive the origin of right from force or from physical necessity.

Proof of the Major:

The Major is evident.

Proof of the Minor:

It is absurd, in the first place, to derive the moral power of binding the wills of others, or the moral obligation to do or omit something, from mere physical necessity. For in that case the right of one becomes stronger and the duties of others become more strict in proportion to the strength of another. It is absurd, in the second place, to derive moral power from non-moral power, and moral obligation from the physical necessity of natural forces.

THIRD PART

The juridical order cannot be derived solely from personal liberty looked at in itself.

Proof

188. The juridical order is essentially connected with the moral order by reason of origin, moral efficacy and its end.

But in the opinion of the opponents, the juridical order, by reason of origin, moral efficacy and end, is totally divorced from morality.

Therefore, the juridical order cannot have its origin solely in personal liberty looked at in itself.

Proof of the Major:

It is clear from the first part of the thesis that the juridical order has its origin from the same principle as the moral order of which it is a part; and hence its moral efficacy cannot be explained otherwise than by recourse to the moral order; likewise it looks to the end which is the object of the moral order.

Proof of the Minor:

(a) In the opinion of the opponents, the juridical order is separated from the moral order by reason of *origin;* for Kant explicitly states that a strict right is that "in which there is no admixture of what is ethical, and which is essentially derived from external and coercive legislative power." (b) The total efficacy of the juridical moral order is, in the same opinion, derived from the power of coercion in the legislator. Nor does it militate against this that Kant declares that juridical duties can at the same time be moral; for this does not belong to them as such, but by reason of the *categorical imperative,* which has no juridical force. (c) The *end* of the juridical order, according to these adversaries, consists totally in the attainment of *external personal liberty;* for external personal liberty, looked at in itself, and absolutely, is the measure and rule of all right.

This part of the thesis is further confirmed by the absurdities which are logically a consequence of this opinion. First of all, practical conclusions must be admitted, which are against public decency and the moral sense of all. For any action, however evil, is, in this opinion, juridical if it preserves the general law of liberty and at the same time is vested with coercive force by the mutual consent of all. In the second place, this opinion admits conclusions that are of their nature harmful to the social order. For from this philosophy of right are logically inferred the primary dogma of modern revolution, the supremacy of the people, the dogma of the idolatry of the state, and the dogma of legal superiority, with the contempt of morality in certain circumstances.

Corollary 1

189. The separation of the juridical order from the moral order rests on these assumptions:

(a) Juridical duty is not determined by the moral law. To this we answer that such a duty can only be determined ultimately by the moral law, although proximately in many cases it is determined by the positive law. Besides, we declare that certain rights are so determined by the moral law, that, apart from any positive law, they can be defended by force. Such are the rights to life and liberty.

(b) This separation of the juridical order from the moral order rests on the assumption that a moral act is not subject to coercion. To this we answer, in the first place, that moral acts are subject to a natural sanction and hence can be subject to the coercion of the positive law in the same way that internal acts are subject to coercion, viz., *indirectly* and mediately. Besides, that an act be subject to coercion can signify, either that the possessor of the right has at the same time the right of employing physical force for the defence of his right or that he has the actual and efficacious power of coercion. Now, the first is conceded ultimately by the Natural Law, and the second does not pertain to the essence of right; nor can the right of coercion be legitimately exercised, even if it is present, unless the first right is at the same time present. Finally, a perfect right has reference solely to the external act from the standpoint of its term. The duty correlative to this right, as *juridical,* looks to the same external act. Hence the subject of the duty is bound by the moral law to place this act, even if the possessor of the right is unable actually and efficaciously to extort it by force.

(c) The third assumption at the basis of this separation of the juridical from the moral order is that the juridical order solely has for its scope the promotion of peace and security in the social life of men and the reconciliation of the personal liberty of each one with the liberty of others. To this we answer that not any kind of peace and security, nor any method of reconciling the liberty of one with the liberty of others, is just. Hence we say that not any order is the object of the juridical order, but that alone which is an external and constituent part of the universal moral order. Finally the question is: What is the basis of the juridical order by reason of which its end is to be determined? It is true, indeed, that a partial end of the juridical order is the preservation of the social liberty of all. Nevertheless, this aim is not the origin of the juridical order, because a reason must be assigned why and how this end is to be attained. Hence it follows that human law, looked at in itself, cannot be the ultimate norm of *justice;* otherwise every human law would be essentially just, there would be no internal distinction between justice and injury founded on rational nature, and legislators could render the unjust just, and prohibit the just, according to the dictates of their free will.

Corollary 2

190. Kant's principle of right, if it be compared with his principle of morality, tends to this, that man is formally emancipated from Divine law and is made an absolute legislator over himself. For in the ethical order, by the autonomy of reason, he is independent of anything external, even God; in the juridical order, he is the framer of his own rights and duties. And so, instead of true juridical order, sanctioned and made inviolable by Divine authority, there is substituted mere legality, supported by physical force. Kant's juridical order is an external mechanism by which, on the analogy of the possibility of the free motions of bodies under the law of the equality of action and reaction, the problem of harmoniously reconciling the coexisting personal liberties of many is solved according to the mathematics of mechanics.

Corollary 3

191. The theory of right, which Fichte defended, is intimately connected with Kant's theory. He likewise declared that external liberty, as the sole connatural right, is the proper philosophical basis of all rights and duties. Kant taught that external liberty

is a postulate of reason, consequent upon internal liberty; Fichte held that it is an essential element of rational nature. This external liberty is, according to the latter, of itself *absolute* and *indeterminate,* but must be restrained by a subjective necessity, viz., *reason,* in order that one's own Ego may be forced to acknowledge other personal entities, enjoying an equal liberty with one's self. Hence there arise the juridical relationship, and at the same time, the rational necessity that each one should restrain his own liberty, in so far as the possibility of the same liberty of others demands. This necessity is called juridical law, which a free being imposes on itself, on this sole condition, that the same thing be done in turn by other beings coexisting with itself. Therefore, every juridical relation exists *determinately,* in so far as it is based on mutual acknowledgment. There is a necessity of free beings associating themselves in community. This is impossible, except by a free compact, by which public civil power is established, which alone by physical and irresistible coercion can reconcile, limit and determine the rights and duties of all and each.

In this opinion, therefore, the *remote* basis of the juridical order is the *original liberty of man, of itself absolute, and without any essential relationship to the Creator, and to be limited,* by reference to the liberty of others. The *proximate* basis of the juridical order is a *mutual pact* by which civil society is constituted. With regard to this we note: (a) How is this original independence, absolute and unlimited, proved? It is not proved to be an essential element of rational nature; indeed, the contrary is proved, where there is question of moral obligation; whatever right man has is subsequent by nature to his duty towards the Creator and hence essentially limited by this duty. (b) Whence comes the necessity of restricting one's own liberty in reference to the liberty of others? Not certainly from autonomous reason, nor from utility as the Utilitarians proclaim. Therefore, it comes from essential duty with regard to God. And so no other original liberty can belong to man than that which is already essentially limited, by reason of which every man, by absolute Divine right, is bound to submit to all those restrictions and modifications of his liberty which are demanded by a predefined and manifest order in the moral world.

TOPICS FOR DISCUSSION

1. Define the juridical order.
2. Distinguish between natural rights and positive rights; between connatural and acquired rights; between alienable and inalienable rights; between jurisdictional and proprietary rights.
3. To what two opinions are all false doctrines on the basis of the juridical order ultimately reducible?

4. What was Hobbes' opinion with regard to the basis of the juridical order? What was Spencer's? What was Kant's?
5. What logical absurdities would be the consequence of Kant's opinion?
6. On what three assumptions does the separation of the juridical from the moral order rest?
7. What is Fichte's opinion with regard to the foundation of the juridical order?
8. How would you explicitly refute Fichte's opinion?

THESIS XXIV

Coercive inviolability is an essential property of perfect right. It is distinct from the physical power efficaciously to exercise coercion. Hence a right remains of itself unimpaired, even if accidentally it is deprived of physical force.

Explanation of the Thesis

192. There are three properties of right, viz., limitation, collision and coercion. Some authors consider the collision of rights under their limitation. *Limitation* is an attribute of right, looked at in itself, viz., a definition of the elements beyond which the right has no efficacy. *Collision* is an attribute of right compared with another right, viz., the apparent opposition of one right to another. *Coercion* is an attribute consequent upon right with regard to another person over whom the right exists. In virtue of coercion, physical might may be brought to compel one to the performance of that to which he is bound by a duty. *Limitation* and *collision* will be treated in a scholion. In the thesis the question is on coercion.

193. *Perfect right* has this peculiar to itself, that it implies not only a moral bond in the proper sense, but, over and above, coercive inviolability. A distinction must be made between the power to coerce and coercion. The power to coerce is the moral power to exercise physical force, if there is need, for the preservation of a right against those who try to prevent its legitimate exercise. Thus, the power to coerce adds a new right to inviolability as such. For inviolability as such regards the moral obligation by which the will of another is bound and always exercises its efficacy *actually*. The power to coerce looks to the physical force to be employed as a means to gain the observance of the right from another. Sometimes it cannot be actually exercised, either because the physical power is not at hand or because in certain circumstances it is more prudent not to exercise it. Hence it follows that the inviolability of the right exercises its power over conscience, but the power to coerce directly over an organism which is

subordinate to the will; that inviolability is irresistible, but the power to coerce is not. Besides, the power to coerce is different from coercion, which is the exercise of physical power.

194. By the common agreement of men, coercive inviolability is understood to belong *intrinsically* and *essentially* to a *perfect right*. The opponents of this thesis, not only agree with us with regard to the *intrinsic* and *essential* connection between right and coercive inviolability, but proceeding further (a) put the right itself in this coercive inviolability which they say is *positive* and *external;* and (b) assert that it belongs to the essential nature of right that it always actually be vested with external efficacy. According to us this coercive power is not that which constitutes a right; but, on the contrary, coercive power belongs to someone, *because* he possesses the right, of which coercive power is an essential consequence.

195. Coercive inviolability implies two things: (a) defense, in order that a right may not be violated; (b) condign punishment, in order that the injury inflicted may be repaired. In other words, the moral power of preserving a right against an injury inflicted, regards the injury, both *in its becoming* and in its *accomplishment*. The object of this moral power is *defense* and *vindication,* in so far as they preserve the mean of virtue.

196. To what subject does coercive power belong?

(a) From the nature of things and considered in itself, the coercive power belongs *primarily* to the same subject in whom is resident the right; it belongs *secondarily* to others who are vicegerents of the primary possessor of the right, viz., a father with regard to his children, public authority with regard to its subjects.

(b) Nevertheless, since the coercive power attached to a right has this purpose that physical force should be a safeguard of the juridical order, the *exercise* of coercive power, or coercion, belongs *primarily* to the subject to whom by natural right the care of the juridical order is entrusted as a special duty. The subject of this duty is civil authority. For if it were licit for any member of civil society arbitrarily to use coercive force for the preservation of his rights, such a use would be harmful to the juridical order. Hence the coercive *power* itself, by the institution of nature, belongs to the individual, but by the same token the *exercise* or *use* of it belongs to civil authority upon which falls the duty of protecting the rights of citizens. From neglect of this distinction, erroneous opinions have arisen by which both the *coercive right* and the *use* of it are entrusted to the public authority as to a primary subject.

However, even in well-ordered society, it can happen that in certain circumstances the right to the exercise of coercive power may return to the subject of the right, viz., a private person, v.g., if there is an instant necessity of self-defense, and recourse to public authority is impossible. For the right to actual coercion belongs to the public authority precisely because coercive inviolability belongs primarily to the individual subject of this right. If, therefore, in cases of urgent necessity, civil society is unable to perform its duty, the right to the use of coercion recurs to the individual.

Finally, if there is a question of civil societies, which as moral personalities are independent of one another, and are subject to no common authority, it is evident that these have both the right and the exercise of coercive power, and that they, within the scope of international law, can defend themselves and redress injuries inflicted upon them.

197. In the last part of the thesis it is asserted that right of itself remains unimpaired even if accidentally either the physical power of coercion or the protection of public authority are not at hand. Therefore, we deny that it belongs to the essential notion of right that it always be vested with external efficacy. We concede, however, and affirm: (a) That the power of effectively exercising coercion is necessary that the real external effect of some rights be safely realized; (b) that it is, therefore, necessary that human society should not be deficient in the public protection of objective justice; (c) and that this provision is a consequence of the natural sociability of man.

The thesis has three parts:

FIRST PART

Coercive inviolability is an essential property of perfect right

Proof

198. One who holds the will of another directly obligated, in order to a real effect, either to be granted, or not impeded, has at the same time the organism, naturally subordinated to that other will indirectly bound to himself, in so far as the instrumental co-operation of this organism is necessary for the effect due him.

But the subject of a right has directly obligated to himself the will of another, in order to a real effect, either to be granted or not impeded.

Therefore, he has bound to himself at the same time the organism subject to this other's will, and consequently may licitly use physical force that the organism be subject to himself, even if the other's will refuse. This is to say that coercive inviolability is an essential property of a perfect right.

The Major and Minor are both evident.

SECOND PART

Coercive inviolability is distinct from the physical power efficaciously to exercise coercion.

Proof

199. If coercive inviolability were not distinct from the physical power efficaciously to exercise coercion, it would be a physical power not only with regard to its exercise, but also with regard to its essence.

But coercive inviolability is essentially moral.

Therefore, coercive inviolability is distinct from the physical power efficaciously to exercise coercion.

Proof of the Major:

A power which is only a power in so far as it has conjoined to itself the material strength efficaciously to exercise coercion is a power physical in its essence. But if coercive inviolability were not distinct from the physical potency to exercise coercion it would be such a power. Therefore, if coercive inviolability were not distinct from the physical power efficaciously to exercise coercion, it would be a physical power not only with regard to exercise, but also with regard to essence.

Proof of the Minor:

Coercive inviolability is in its essence a power which implies in its subject the right of licit coercion and in its term a duty which can be licitly extorted. But such a power is essentially moral. Therefore, coercive inviolability is essentially moral.

THIRD PART

A right remains of itself unimpaired even if accidentally it is deprived of physical force.

Proof

200. Although an external condition, which only touches the exercise of a right is accidentally absent, the right remains of itself unimpaired.

But physical force is an external condition of right, which only touches the exercise of the right.

Therefore, the right remains of itself unimpaired, even if accidentally it is deprived of its physical force.

Proof of the Major:

Right is moral power and its exercise is its external and final complement, not something constituting the right as such. But if an external condition is accidentally absent, which only touches this complement of right, the right of itself remains unimpaired. Therefore, even if there is accidentally absent an external condition which only touches the exercise of the right, the right of itself remains unimpaired.

Proof of the Minor:

A power which in its essence is not moral power, and which, nevertheless, is required for the external efficacy of a moral power or right, is an external condition which only touches its exercise. But such a power is physical force. Therefore, physical force is an external condition of right, which only touches its exercise.

The third part of the thesis is confirmed by the absurdities which would follow if a right should cease when physical power accidentally ceased. For it is absurd: (a) that the rights of men in their essence and their juridical binding power should depend upon uncertain, varying and accidental conditions; (b) that the rights of men can be obliterated through the arbitrary will of evil and stronger men; (c) that the rights of men could arise by injustice. Such absurdities would follow if the rights of men were obliterated merely because there was wanting the protection, either private or public, of physical force.

Scholion

The limitation and collision of rights and duties

201. *Limitation* is the defining of the boundaries beyond which moral power has no efficacy in rights and duties, either in relation to the term of the right, or to the subject of the duty. Every human right, whether it be an individual or social right, inasmuch as it is participated, is by its very nature limited. This limitation comes in the first place from the *purpose* of right; for the purpose or end is the measure of things which have reference to the purpose or end. But the end, as we have already noted, is either *ultimate* or *proximate, spiritual* or *temporal*. He who has a right to an end has the right to those means without which the end cannot be attained. In the second place, the right is limited by the *matter* with which the right is concerned, and this is determined by the *title*. In the third place, right is limited by the *juridical duty* of men *towards God,* in virtue of which a temporal end, and the means to it, and the matter with which the right is concerned, can be limited. To these limits of right correspond similar limitations in the duties which are the correlatives of right.

202. *Collision* of rights and duties. Rights and duties are said to collide when they are in such conflict that it is impossible to satisfy simultaneously both. Since every right, just as every duty, is ultimately based on Natural Law, it is certain that there can be no *objectively real* collision of rights and duties. The collision is only apparent. For the Natural Law cannot at the same time either ratify or command things which are mutually repugnant. Hence the solution of this collision consists in dissipating the appearance of conflict and thus determining which right or duty according to correct reason *prevails* over another. Hence we ask: (a) What should be our attitude, if two rights with regard to the same matter appear in conflict; (b) what should be our attitude if two urgent duties appear *incompatible?*

Collision of rights. The question refers, as is evident, to rights which belong to different subjects. There is no question with regard to conflicts concerning certain positive rights which can be solved by the civil courts. Our question is not one of jurisprudence, but of ethics, for the solution of which we propose, (a) certain general principles and (b) particular rules.

(a) *General principles.* In the first place, since every right is granted by law, the right must be interpreted in the light of the limitations which explicitly or implicitly are contained in the law. Sometimes it happens that a right is conceived, as granted by a law looked at in general, when the exceptions, which are rationally implied in the moral power, are not expressed. Hence arises an apparent conflict of rights, which in reality has its origin in an imperfect apprehension of the extent of a right.

In the second place, although the right is constituted by Natural Law, nevertheless it can happen that such a right in certain conditions is suspended in its actual exercise although it remains unimpaired in itself. In other words, a right absolutely looked at can exist, but *relatively* to certain conditions the use of it is not conceded.

(b) *Particular rules.* It does not seem possible to set up rules which have universal application, so that they imply no exceptions. For the variety of conditions which are the source of an apparent conflict of rights is such that oftentimes we can only say, that the matter is to be decided from the elements of right, viz., from its basis, matter, title, subject and term. To these can be added the purpose for which the right is conceded by Natural Law. Nevertheless, the following rules are presented which have a general, though not a universal, validity:

(1) An inalienable right can never be in conflict with another inalienable right; for it cannot happen that two rights are in conflict which can neither licitly nor validly be renounced. For if this could happen, the conflict would be based on the Natural Law itself, which is impossible.

(2) An inalienable right *per se* prevails over every alienable right, as is manifest from the very concept of these two kinds of right.

(3) A connatural right *per se, other things being equal,* prevails over an acquired right. This rule, however, is not very useful, since *the other things* are rarely equal.

(4) A right based on Natural Law, if it is alienable, sometimes yields to a right founded on positive law. The reason is because the positive law determines with certitude for concrete circumstances that which is oftentimes left indeterminate by the Natural Law. However, if the natural right is certain and determinate, it *per se* prevails over a positive right.

203. *Collision of duties.* Prescinding from negative duties between which there can be no collision, three things are especially to be considered in the determination of the duty which prevails in a conflict of duties:

(1) The *principle* from which the duty arises. The duty is more grave in accordance with the importance and strictness of the law which imposes the obligation. Such a duty prevails over a less grave duty.

(2) The *matter* with which the duty is concerned. Hence duties which touch a supreme good must be preferred to others; in the same way the common good is to be preferred to a private good; and a good more necessary to a good less necessary.

(3) The *term* with regard to which duties exist. Hence duties towards God prevail over duties towards men. Nevertheless, if these duties are affirmative and can be postponed, they

ought often to be postponed, if there are certain negative duties towards ourselves or others to be satisfied. The same thing may be said towards duties towards ourselves and towards others in an apparent conflict. But if there is question of duties of charity towards others, the order of preference is *per se* to be determined from the relationship of the term of the duty to ourselves.

TOPICS FOR DISCUSSION

1. What are the three properties of right? Define each.
2. What do you mean by the coercive inviolability of right?
3. Why is it true that might cannot be the basis of right?
4. Who is the primary subject of coercive inviolability?
5. Who is the primary subject of coaction?
6. What general and what particular principles may we apply for the solving of an apparent collision of rights or duties?
7. Apply these principles to the two following cases:

I.

A soldier in a time of war is keeping sentry duty near a lake. In this lake he sees a boy in proximate danger of death from drowning, and doubts whether it is lawful for him to leave his post for a brief moment to rescue the boy. Although at the present moment there is no immediate danger from the enemy, the precept of not leaving the sentry post was imposed under penalty of death. In this case the positive precept imposed on the soldier seems stronger than the natural duty to rescue a human being in danger of death; first, because it is a negative precept and hence binds always and for always; secondly, because the common good should be preferred to the private good of the drowning boy. On the other hand, it seems to the soldier, who is well versed in matters of ethics, that the duty of charity being a natural duty and in this case immediately urgent, prevails over the positive precept to remain at his assigned post. Besides, it seems to him, that in the present circumstances the common good is not jeopardized; but that this solely can come under consideration, whether it is lawful for him to subject his own life to the danger of the death penalty to save the life of another. What do you think the soldier ought to do and is allowed to do in these circumstances?

II.

A young man of absolute innocence is accused and condemned to perpetual imprisonment by the evil machinations of a rival. On one occasion, there was offered to him the assured opportunity of escape. This he was unwilling to use because, although aware of his natural right to recover his liberty, he thought that this right was subordinate to the public right, which had been confirmed by juridical decision. However, after a long time in prison, he perceives that there is present a great danger to his moral well-being, because of his daily association with many pernicious criminals. And so when the opportunity to escape is again offered, he makes use of it without any hesitation, in the assurance that his inalienable right to moral integrity prevails over all other rights. To assure his escape, he seizes the Rolls-Royce of his unjust accuser and by its aid safely crosses the Mexican boundary. Here he sells the Rolls-Royce and uses the money for his support. What do you think of the reasons which the young man used through this wholly fictitious case?

READINGS FOR CHAPTER X

Adversaria Ethica, Timothy J. Brosnahan, S.J.

Glenn, part ii, "Rights and Duties," chap. i, pp. 135-151.

Ross, Book II, chap. iv, p. 241.

Poland, "Rights," chap. ix, pp. 96-101; "Duties," chap. x, pp. 101-106; "Collision of Rights," chap. xi, pp. 106-118; "Vindication of Rights," chap. xii, pp. 118-123.

Leibell, pp. 405-427.

Cronin, "On Rights," chap. xx, pp. 660-686.

LeBuffe, "Rights and Duties or Effect of Law," sect. vii, pp. 72-84.

Holaind, "Conflict of Rights," chap. x, pp. 265-287.

Keane, "Rights," part iii, chap. iv, p. 147.

Rickaby, part ii, chap. v, "Of Rights," pp. 244-263.

CHAPTER XI

THESIS XXV

Character is an integration of habits of conduct superimposed on temperament. Character is morally perfect, when it results from the combined and harmonized virtues, which determine our ethical and juridical duties to God, to our neighbor, and in respect to ourselves.

Introduction

204. In previous theses, we have established the general principles of morally good or right living. In this thesis, we point out the result of living according to those principles; the result is a morally perfect character. Character has been well defined as "Life dominated by principle." It is a personality, the thoughts, words and actions of which are guided and ruled by those standards of living, that flow from all man's relations to God, to the neighbor and to self.

N.B.—This thesis hardly admits of a formal proof. It needs merely to be explained to have its truth appear.

Explanation

205. *Character* etymologically means a significant mark stamped or cut on a hard material. Thence it is applied to a combination of qualities distinguishing one individual or group of individuals from others. The notion, therefore, varies with the science that employs it. Ethically, character means the sum of moral traits or qualities which distinguish a *person* or *class of persons* from others, and by reason of which they receive a special moral designation. The qualities which individuate personality coalesce in two syntheses: *temperament* due to *nature* and *character* due to *nurture*.

206. Temperament is the fusion of the various dispositions of our composite nature into a resultant *disposition* of the whole man. *Disposition* is a native bent towards action of a certain kind, and capacity for a certain form or development. In a secondary sense, it is a tendency that has been awakened by previous workings of bent, without, however, giving formed capacity; so understood, it is the initial factor of *habit* in formation. *Habit* is a quality superinduced in a faculty by repeated performance of its functions, giving an *impulse* to an *ease* in the exercise of these functions. Therefore, *habits* and *dispositions* differ. Dispositions are *congenital* and *plastic,* i.e., are receptive of form through use, and liable to degeneracy from disuse. Habits are *acquired* and *stable,* i.e., once fixed, they can be thrown off only by the continued exercise of contrary acts.

207. Habits of our rational nature are of two kinds:

(1) *Habits of thought,* i.e., of intellect. These invigorate intellectual dispositions and determine them in a particular direction, and are the products of disposition and training.

(2) *Habits of conduct,* i.e., of will. These, which may be either good or bad, confer impulse and ease in the active determination of the will to appropriate ends, and are the product of will freely exercised on disposition, thought, emotion and action.

N.B.—*Morally good habits,* prompting to right action, which is another way of saying the performance of duty, are called virtues. *Morally bad habits,* in like manner, prompting to wrong action, which is another way of saying the violation of duty, are called *vices.* What dispositions are to temperament, habits of conduct are to character. As the mental constitution due to the fusion of the former is *temperament,* so the blending of the latter into a unitary principle is *character.*

Character, therefore, is an integration of habits of conduct superimposed on temperament.

208. The question now arises: "When is our character morally perfect?" The thesis answers: When it results from good habits of conduct or virtues, combined and harmonized, which prompt a man to abide by his duties both merely ethical and juridical to God, to the neighbor and in respect to ourselves.

The term duty, as we have seen, is used in two senses: (1) In a *comprehensive* sense to signify moral necessity of any kind, and in this sense it is the immediate effect of *objective* right; (2) in a *restricted* sense to signify the moral necessity of doing something in favor of another, and in this sense it is the immediate effect of a *subjective* right. All duty, in its last analysis, is the duty of obeying the Supreme Legislator. Duties regard different object-parties, though the object-party is always a person, viz., an intelligent being. We have duties *concerning* inanimate or animate beings; and, as they rise in the grade of being, our duties *concerning* them become more intensive, but we have no duties *to* them. Now intellectual beings are in two categories, created and uncreated; and created being is either self or others. The object-parties of duties, therefore, are God, self and our neighbors. Duties are *natural* or *positive; affirmative* or *negative; merely ethical* or *jurid-*

ical. The former in the last division is based on charity and the allied virtues and the latter on commutative justice.

Duties to God:

Virtues determine the attitude of man's intellect and will to God. The virtues which fundamentally secure this are those by which man is prompted to seek knowledge of God, and to give Him intellectual submission, to love Him above all things, and to desire final union with Him. These comprise wisdom, charity and hope. To these must be added the virtue of religion, by which man is prompted to worship and honor God because of His infinite excellence, absolute dominion and supreme goodness.

Duties to the Neighbor:

In relation to the neighbor, individually or collectively, the virtues of the morally perfect character will be *benevolence* and *justice,* by which the will is prompted to wish others well, and to render to everyone his due. *Justice* is divided into: (a) *Social* or *legal,* between the *individual* and the *state.* This *duty* is in the *individual subject,* the duty to perform that which by natural or state law is for common good. The *right* is in the state. (b) Distributive, between the *state* and the *individual citizen.* This *duty* is in the state to distribute social burdens and benefits in proportional equality, e.g., taxes. The *right* is in the *individual* as a citizen. (c) Commutative, between private individuals. This *duty* is in *each man* towards his *fellowman,* to render to him what is his private exclusive property. This *right* is also in *each man* as a man.

Duties in respect to Ourselves:

In relation to ourselves, the virtues of the morally perfect character will be: (1) *prudence,* which gives a readiness and ease in the right use of practical reason; (2) *temperance,* which moderates the passions that allure to sensuous delight; (3) *fortitude,* which controls the passions that arouse fear or impel to rashness in the presence of impending loss or threatening danger. The morally perfect character, then, will have all the virtues which relate to God, to self, and to the neighbor, and the virtues which are intrinsically allied to these, viz., abstinence, sobriety, chastity, humility, meekness, modesty, magnanimity, patience, obedience, truthfulness, etc. A character so constituted is conformed to rational nature in all its essential relations, and is, therefore, a *morally perfect character.*

READINGS FOR CHAPTER XI

Theses in General Ethics, Fordham University Press.
The Formation of Character, Ernest R. Hull, S.J.

LIST OF THESES

LIST OF BOOKS FOR ADVISED READING

Catholic Encyclopedia, Encyclopedia Press, Inc., New York.

Political and Moral Essays, Joseph Rickaby, S.J., Benziger Brothers, New York.

Ethica, Charles V. Lamb, S.J., Woodstock College Press, Woodstock, Md.

Ethica, Marcellus Nivard, S.J., Gabriel Beauchesne, Paris, France.

Ethics, Paul J. Glenn, Ph.D., S.T.D., B. Herder Book Company, St. Louis, Mo.

Adversaria Ethica, Timothy J. Brosnahan, S.J., Woodstock College Press, Woodstock, Md.

Christian Ethics, J. Elliot Ross, Devin-Adair Company, New York.

The Formation of Character, Ernest R. Hull, S.J., B. Herder Book Company, New York.

Fundamental Ethics, William Poland, Silver, Burdett & Company, New York.

General Ethics, Joseph F. Sullivan, S.J., Holy Cross College Press, Worcester, Mass.

Theses in General Ethics, Fordham University Press, New York.

A Historical Introduction to Ethics, Thomas Verner Moore, Ph.D., American Book Company, New York.

De Ethica Naturali, C. Macksey, S.J., Gregorian University, Rome, Italy.

Readings in Ethics, J. F. Leibell, Ph.D., Loyola University Press, Chicago, Ill.

Science of Ethics, Rev. Michael Cronin, M.A., D.D., Benziger Brothers, New York.

Ethica Generalis, Joseph Donat, S.J., Innsbruck, Austria.

Institutiones Juris Naturalis, Theodore Meyer, S.J., Herder & Co., Freiburg, Germany.

Outlines of Pure Jurisprudence, Francis P. LeBuffe, S.J., Fordham University Press, New York.

Natural Law and Legal Practice, Rene I. Holaind, S.J., Benziger Brothers, New York.

A Primer of Moral Philosophy, Rev. Henry Keane, S.J., M.A., P. J. Kenedy & Sons, New York.

Philosophia Moralis, Victor Cathrein, S.J., Herder & Company, Freiburg, Germany.

History of Philosophy, William Turner, S.T.D., Ginn and Company, New York.

Moral Philosophy, Joseph Rickaby, S.J., Benziger Brothers, New York.

Psychology, Michael Maher, S.J., Longmans, Green & Co., New York.

The Freedom of Science, Joseph Donat, S.J., D.D., Joseph F. Wagner, New York.

The Limitations of Science, J. W. N. Sullivan, The Viking Press, New York.

The Religion of Scientists, C. L. Drawbridge, M.A., The Macmillan Company, New York.

Survivals and New Arrivals, Hilaire Belloc, The Macmillan Company, New York.

Why Should I Be Moral?, Ernest R. Hull, S.J., P. J. Kenedy & Sons, New York.

Summa Theologica, Contra Gentiles, Quæstiones Disputatæ, St. Thomas.

APPENDIX

INTRODUCTION

It is universally recognized by men that there is a difference between right and wrong in man's free or volitional actions, that in consequence there are some actions which man ought not to perform, some which he ought to perform, some which he may perform or omit just as he pleases. This universal judgment (recognition) of men is expressed very frequently in propositions such as these: "The moral law forbids such an action." "The moral law commands such an action." "The moral law permits such an action." We will choose one definite example of the application of each of these general propositions and then by a series of questions and answers try to make clear just what is meant by, and all that is implied in the expressions: "prohibitions—commands—permissions of the moral law." Let the following be the examples, chosen because their truth is so evident that they are admitted without question by all men of reason:

1. The moral law forbids a false oath.
2. The moral law commands the worship of God.
3. The moral law permits the use of animals as food.

Q. 1.—What is meant by saying that an action is forbidden or commanded or permitted by the moral law?

A. 1.—That *God,* man's creator, *wills* either the action to be omitted (if forbidden) or performed (if commanded) or left to the choice of the human agent (if permitted).

Q. 2.—How can we show as a purely philosophical conclusion—i.e., a conclusion formed by reason without any help from the teachers of revealed religion—that God does will the omission or performance of any particular volitional action and that He has not left them all to the free choice of the human agent?

A. 2.—By proving that it was *necessary* for God to will the omission or performance of some action in particular.

    N.B.—Q.—Is it proper to say that God is necessitated to any act with regard to a creature?

        A.—Yes, if we mean, as we do here, that He was *hypothetically necessitated,* i.e., that it was necessary for Him so to act in the hypothesis or supposition that He freely determined to create.

Q. 3.—How can we prove this hypothetical necessity of God's willing the omission or performance of any particular volitional action?

A. 3.—By proving that the action in question is such (of such a nature) that in the first case its performance, in the second case its omission is not in harmony with the NORM OF MORALITY.

    N.B.—(1) What is meant by the norm of morality?

        A.—By NORM is meant A RULE with which to measure or a STANDARD by which to judge.

        By NORM OF MORALITY, therefore, is meant a RULE with which to measure or a STANDARD by which to judge MORALITY.

(2) What is meant by Morality?

A.—A quality that makes a man's action either destructive or perfective of the nature of the human agent.

(3) What names are given to these different qualities of a human action?

A.—MORAL GOODNESS OR MORAL BADNESS —*goodness* or *badness* from the general use of these terms to signify the suitableness or convenience (perfectiveness) and unsuitableness or inconvenience (destructiveness) of one thing with regard to another, and *moral* goodness or badness because there is question of the suitableness or unsuitableness of an action to man's nature which is a moral nature. By a moral nature is meant a nature that is intelligent and free and therefore capable of self-directed and self-determined action.

THEREFORE—By NORM OF MORALITY is meant a rule with which to measure or a standard by which to judge the moral goodness or badness of human actions.

(4) In reality, what is this rule or standard, this norm?

A.—PROXIMATELY (i.e., nearest to the action itself), it is rational nature, considered exactly as it is in itself and in all the essential relationships in which it stands with regard to God, fellowmen and irrational creatures;

REMOTELY (i.e., that on which the proximate standard itself depends), it is God's own nature.

(5) How can this last answer be proved?

A.—By a mere explanation of the terms "good" and "bad" as applied to volitional actions. They mean, as always, suitable or unsuitable, and actions of any agent can be said to be suitable or unsuitable only with reference to (or considered in relation to) the *agent* performing them. Hence volitional actions can be said to be suitable or unsuitable (good or bad) only with reference to the nature of the *human* agent, and this is a rational but composite nature, with very definite *essential* relations towards God, fellowmen and irrational creatures. Hence the proximate (nearest) measure, standard or norm of goodness or badness (morality) of volitional actions is man's rational nature and actions which are suitable to (in harmony with) this nature are evidently *good* —*morally* good because man's nature is, as has been said, a moral nature—and vice versa, actions that are unsuitable to (not in harmony with) are *bad* and *morally* bad.

Now this rational nature (the proximate norm of morality) is what it is only because, like every other created nature, it is a particular imitation of the Divine Nature. The Divine Nature is the exemplar and model according to which all created natures have been formed and fashioned and must, in consequence, be the model and exemplar according to which all creatures' actions must be ultimately conformed, if they are to be ultimately—in the last analysis—suitable (good). Hence the ultimate (farthest removed) measure or standard or norm of goodness or badness (morality) of volitional actions is that on which the proximate norm (man's rational nature) ultimately depends and that is the Divine Nature.

Q. 4.—What, therefore, is meant by saying that a volitional action is *such* that in the first case its performance, and in the second its omission, is not in harmony with the NORM OF MORALITY? (In other words, EXPLAIN the answer to Question 3.)

A. 4.—Simply this, that the action is such that in the first case its performance, in the second case its omission, does not befit (is not suitable to) the rational nature of man. For example: (1) A false oath is such that its performance does not befit—is not suitable to—does not fit in with (cf. "convenient" from the Latin *"conveniens,"* which is from the verb *"convenire,"* which is compounded of *"CUM"* and *"VENIRE,"* i.e., to "come or go along with.")—the nature of man. The reason is that the nature of man is essentially so dependent upon God, his Creator, that only actions that do God no dishonor fit in with or are suitable to that nature. But a false oath does God dishonor.

(2) The worship of God is an action such that its total and constant omission does not befit—is not in harmony with—the nature of man. The reason happens to be the same in this case as in the first example, viz., that the nature of man is so essentially dependent upon God, his Creator, for its very existence and for all its powers of action, etc., that the total and constant omission on man's part of the worship of God does not fit in with—is not suitable to—that nature.

(WORSHIP OF GOD means the acknowledgment of God's infinite excellence and supreme dominion over His creatures, and the manifestation towards Him, in consequence of His excellence and dominion, of special reverence, service and love.)

Q. 5.—How does the fact that an action can thus be proved to be such that its performance or omission is out of harmony with the norm of morality, how does this fact show that God was hypothetically necessitated to will (command) its omission or performance? (In other words, PROVE the answer given to Question 3.)

A. 5.—This fact (viz., that an act is such, etc.) shows that the action in question is such that its performance in the first case, its omission in second, will tend not to the perfection, but to the deterioration (destruction) of the agent. And since God must wish (command) the attainment of, not the loss of, the agent's perfection, He must also wish (command) the omission in the first place and the performance in the second of the action as a necessary means to this end.

Q. 6.—Why must God wish the attainment of the agent's perfection?

A. 6.—Because only by the attainment of the agent's perfection can God's purpose in creating that agent be attained, viz., God's external glory.

N.B.—(1) How can it be proved that God had a purpose in creating?

> **A.**—It can be proved from God's infinite intelligence and wisdom. Such a being must have a purpose in acting.

(2) How can it be proved in Cosmology? Cf. Coppens' *Moral Philosophy*, p. 17.

(3) Why must God wish the attainment of His purpose in creating?

> **A.**—Because of the constancy of His purpose, the unchangeableness of His will. Not to wish it would be to be guilty of fickleness.

Q. 7.—How can it be proved that the attainment of God's external glory requires the attainment of the perfection of the creature's nature? (In other words, PROVE the answer given to Question 6.)

A. 7.—(A) In general with regard to any and every creature:

The attainment of God's external glory requires the attainment of the perfection of the creature's nature because the created nature is the particular means employed by an all-wise and powerful Creator to secure this very thing—His external glory. Considering the Creator's wisdom and power, we must argue that the created nature, with its special kind and extent of powers of action, was chosen precisely as the proper and exactly proper means to secure this particular end. But powers of acting secure the end, for which they were created, only by acting, and they secure the last end for which they were created only by acting up to their capacity. Now by acting up to this full capacity, the agent, of which they are the powers, attains its own perfection. Therefore, the attainment of the end for which an all-wise Creator has created a nature demands the attainment on the part of the created nature of its own perfection.

(B) In *particular* with regard to *man:*

The attainment of God's FORMAL external glory—viz., His external glory in the real, true and strictest sense of the word—requires the attainment of the perfection of *man's* nature because this real formal glory consists exactly in the perfect knowledge which man, God's rational creature, has of God's goodness and perfection and the consequent perfect love of and praise of the same on man's part. But this perfect knowledge and love of God, man's absolutely last end and supreme good, constitutes exactly man's ultimate intrinsic perfection. Therefore, the attainment by man of God's external glory requires the attainment of man's perfection.

N.B.—(1) What is this ultimate intrinsic perfection of man called?

> **A.**—Blessedness.

(2) Why is it so called?

> **A.**—Because man's nature, as a conscious nature, must, upon attaining its perfection, experience the *subjective pleasurable emotion* that every conscious faculty experiences upon the attainment of its proper object. That a conscious faculty does experience such emotion in such a case is known to us in our own case from our own internal experience (consciousness) and in the case of other men from their way of acting as well as from their own explicit testimony and in the case of animals from their way of acting.

Now such *subjective pleasurable emotion* is in general called PLEASURE, which may be defined: THE VITAL SATISFACTION OF DESIRE. Desire is a conscious tendency, and the satisfaction experienced upon the attainment of the object, towards which the tendency is directed, is the subjective pleasurable emotion.

And since man's nature (as shown by and exercising itself or "functioning" through his supreme and *specifically characteristic* tendency, viz., his will) has a desire without limit—for all that is desirable—for ALL GOOD (Cf. Treatise on Will in Psychology)—the attainment of its perfection (the fulfilment of such a desire) will be the VITAL SATISFACTION OF ALL DESIRE. And to this kind of pleasure is given the name of HAPPINESS.

Therefore, just as the intrinsic perfection of every nature consists in the state of complete subjective well-being of that nature, so in the case of man it can consist in nothing else than the state of complete subjective well-being of man. And this state of well-being can consist of nothing else than the perfect and unending possession through intellect and will of an object capable of meeting and satisfying man's unlimited desire and, therefore, his unlimited powers of *enjoying* satisfaction. And such a possession of such an object will fulfil this unlimited desire and in consequence give to man that vital satisfaction of all desire which we call HAPPINESS.

AND TO THIS STATE OF COMPLETE WELL-BEING OF MAN'S LIFE AND ACTIVITY WITH THE HAPPINESS NECESSARILY CONSEQUENT THEREUPON IS GIVEN THE NAME—BLESSEDNESS.

(3) How can it be proved that the attainment of this state of BLESSEDNESS is possible to man?

A.—It can be proved from the infinite goodness and truthfulness of the Creator Who implanted in man's nature the craving—conscious tendency—for it.

Q. 8.—But how can we determine in *particular* what actions of man are in harmony with, what others are not in harmony with the norm of morality?

A. 8.—By considering that which gives every action its own peculiar and distinctive nature, viz., its *formal* object. (Cf. "Acts are *specified* by their *formal* objects.")

Q. 9.—Describe what is understood in general by the formal object of a volitional act?

A. 9.—The formal object is that which, as represented by the intellect, terminates here and now the tendency of the will's act of desiring or choosing. In other words, it is the full and complete and exact answer to the question, *"What* is it that the *will wants* here and now?" Notice that we say "as represented by the intellect" because the will cannot really wish here and now what the man willing does not here and now really know. (Cf. *"Nil volitum nisi præcognitum."*) Therefore, though a man can freely tend by an act of his will towards a certain object which has certain qualities, he does not really tend towards those qualities unless while tending he *knows* them, i.e., although those qualities are really in the object desired or chosen, they do not enter into the real (formal) object of that act of desiring or choosing (though they do enter into what is called the material object), and so do not play any part in determining (or specifying) the nature of that act of tending or desiring or choosing.

Q. 10.—What *more particularly* are the factors that make up the formal object of any volitional act and so determine whether said act is or is not in harmony with the norm of morality? In other words, what elements must be enumerated in a full, complete and exact answer to the question, "What is it that the will wants here and now?"

A. 10.—These factors or elements are three in number, viz., the End of Action, the End of Agent and the Circumstances intrinsically affecting either.

Q. 11.—How can this answer be proved?

A. 11.—By an analysis of a volitional act. For when a man deliberately chooses (determines himself to) a particular action, he chooses it—

(1) Because it is what it is, an act of this particular nature, an act normally issuing in some particular end or result; that is to say, he chooses it as, *and because it is,* an action which has of its nature some particular end, i.e., he wants this *End of Action;*

(2) Because it is a means to some other end of his own choice; that is to say, he chooses it as, *and because it is,* an action which will obtain for him the end he sets for himself in acting, i.e., he wants also this end of his or this *End of Agent;*

(3) As it is in all the definite *Circumstances* of person acting, person or thing acted upon, of time, place, manner, etc.

Hence if there be any moral evil in the tendency of the will in any given action it must be due to the fact that in one or two or all of these three elements, constituting the object of that tendency, there is seen to be something that is unfitting for man's nature to tend towards.

N.B.—(1) May the End of Action and End of Agent in any particular action be identical?

A.—In the case of an Infinite Agent they *must* be identical. In the case of finite agents, they *may* be identical or distinct. When they are identical, then the morality of the action in question is not modified by the End of Agent in any other way than it is determined by the End of Action.

(2) How should actions which are morally good or bad from End of Action be designated?

A.—They should be said to be *intrinsically* and of their *very nature* good or bad.

(3) Is it not, therefore, true that, if any particular volitional act is known to be intrinsically good or bad, no further investigation is needed in order to judge the morality of that act?

A.—We must distinguish: (a) If any act is known to be intrinsically *bad,* no further investigation is needed in order to be sure that that act is, always was, and always will be, bad, no matter what the End of the Agent placing it be nor under what circumstances it be placed. However, even in such a case, a further investigation of the other two elements is required in order to determine the exact degree of moral evil the action would have in any given concrete case. For the essential evil attaching to the act from its nature (End of Action) might be aggravated by the End of Agent or by some of the Circumstances and might also by the same be mitigated to an extent, though never so far as to have its essential morality changed and itself become a good action.

(b) If any act is known to be intrinsically *good,* further investigation is needed before one can be sure of the morality of the act as actually placed. For every volitional action in its concrete performance involves some End of Agent and a number of concrete circumstances and any one of these elements may render an action, which of its nature is good, here and now unfitting or bad.

N.B.—The doctrine expressed in this answer is summarized in the axiom, *"Bonum ex integra causa, malum ex quocumque defectu."*

(4) Since the answer to Questions 3 and 4 state that it is the relationship of harmony or discord between a man's action and rational nature which gives to that action its morality, what is the proper way to designate these three elements treated of in the two foregoing questions?

A.—They should be called the *specific* determinants of moral good and evil. For, although all good actions are alike *generically* inasmuch as they are in harmony with the norm and all bad actions are alike *generically* inasmuch as they are not in harmony with the same, it is due to these three elements that any action has its *particular* kind or *species* of harmony or discord.

Q. 12.—Can the main points of doctrine contained in the foregoing eleven questions and answers be stated in one sentence?

A. 12.—Yes, as follows: "God wishes men in their conduct (volitional actions) to attain their intrinsic perfection (Blessedness) and thus accomplish His purpose in creating (His external glory) by performing only those actions that are in *every* way (i.e., considering End of Action *and* End of Agent *and* Circumstances) in harmony with his (man's) nature, and by avoiding all actions that are in *any* way (i.e., considering End of Action *or* End of Agent *or* Circumstances) out of harmony with his nature."

Q. 13.—Is not this statement substantially equivalent to the universal judgment and to the threefold proposition mentioned in the Introduction of this Summary?

A. 13.—It is.

Q. 14.—How can this be shown to be so?

A. 14.—As follows: The statement contained in Answer 12 involves these propositions:

(1) There is a rule for man's volitional actions.

(2) This rule has been established by man's superior (God).

(3) This rule has been promulgated (made known) to man.

(4) This rule is promulgated as mandatory upon man's free will.

(5) This rule has been established and promulgated by God for the good of the universe He has created.

But a "rule of action, mandatory in form, established and promulgated by a superior (competent authority) for a common good" is exactly what is universally expressed by the term "*Law.*"

Hence we may express all that is contained in Answer 12 by saying: "God's law commands some actions, forbids others, permits others."

Further, since this law of God deals with man's free (or moral) actions and its binding force is brought to bear upon his will through his intellect (faculties distinctive of a moral nature), it is naturally called the "*Moral* Law."

Hence the expression: "The Moral Law commands, forbids, permits certain actions."

Q. 15.—What other name is frequently given to this moral law, and why?

A. 15.—It is frequently called the *natural law* (1) because of the method of its promulgation, viz., through the *very nature* of the subjects it binds, (2) because its prescriptions and prohibitions are also necessarily determined by the *nature* of its subjects—for it is, as we have seen, this nature that is the norm of the subject's good or bad actions.

Q. 16.—What are some of the chief characteristics of this natural moral law?

A. 16.—(1) Its *immutability,* which denies the possibility of its precepts being changed, abrogated or dispensed from;

(2) Its *knowability,* which denies that its most general principles and their simplest application can be invincibly unknown to the normal man in average social conditions;

(3) Its *insufficiency,* which demands that it be supplemented by positive law.

Q.—What is meant by positive law?

A.—Positive Law is a rule of action *freely* established by competent authority and promulgated *not* in the nature of its subject, but by some external (oral or written) sign or expression.

Positive law, therefore, receives its binding power ultimately from the natural law and must itself proceed from legitimate authority, be just, possible and properly promulgated.

(4) Its need of adequate and proportioned sanction as means to secure its observance and prevent its violation. This need the natural moral law has in common with all real laws.

> N.B.—(1) In what does this sanction of the natural moral law consist?
>
> > A.—It consists in the realization or frustration of the final perfection of man's rational nature and can be had therefore only in a future life.

Q. 17.—Through what faculty of man's nature are the precepts of the Natural Moral Law made known (promulgated)?

A. 17.—Through man's intellect.

Q. 18.—What, then, is understood by the term "Conscience"?

A. 18.—Conscience is a term used to designate *either* the Intellect as the faculty capable of judging the moral quality of volitional actions, *or* (more commonly and more properly) the ACT of the intellect making some such judgment whether about morality of actions in the abstract or in the concrete; OR (in the *most proper* sense) the last practical judgment of the intellect regarding the moral goodness or badness of an action here and now to be performed.

Q. 19.—Does the intellect, studying the nature of man and itself as an essential faculty of that nature, discover any rules which must be followed in order that in its own functioning as "conscience" it prove a safe and correct guide?

A. 19.—Yes, as follows:

(1) A prudentially certain conscience must be obeyed, even when *invincibly* erroneous.

(2) To act with a doubtful conscience is never lawful.

(3) In cases in which doubts cannot be solved directly, a prudentially certain conscience can be formed by the use of reflex principles.

Q. 20.—What are the prescriptions and prohibitions of the Natural Moral Law commonly called?

A. 20.—Natural *Duties,* either affirmative or negative.

Q. 21.—What follows immediately from the existence of these *natural* duties?

A. 21.—It follows that man has from natural law also the *means* necessary to fulfil these duties.

Q. 22.—What are the most important of these means?

A. 22.—*First,* the *power* to restrain others from such interference with one's activity as would make it impossible or unreasonably difficult for one to fulfil one's natural duties;

Second, the *power* to obtain, hold and use for oneself whatever is required for the fulfilment of these same duties.

Q. 23.—Are the *physical* powers given man by nature sufficient to enable him to accomplish the foregoing?

A. 23.—Evidently not. Some other kind of power must also be given man by nature.

Q. 24.—What is the other kind of power called, and why?

A. 24.—It is called a *moral* power—because the only other kind of power besides physical that can conceivably aid man is the power to influence in such a way the *wills* of other men that these may be led to *determine themselves freely—*

(1) not to interfere with a fellowman's above-mentioned requisite freedom, and

(2) to permit fellowman to obtain, hold and make undisturbed use of whatever the natural law makes it lawful or obligatory for him to demand. Now—the only way in which such influence can be brought to bear upon the *free-will* of others is by proposing to their *intellects* motives that will serve to *induce* on their part this *self-determined* restraint. And a power that is exercised upon free wills through intellectual knowledge is rightly called a *MORAL POWER.*

Q. 25.—What is the motive that is proposed by nature to influence in this way the will of others?

A. 25.—The evidence that something is by nature so connected with some person as a necessary or lawful means to the fulfilment of that person's natural duties that another's refusal to permit him to obtain, hold or use the thing would be itself an act out of harmony with rational nature and, therefore, a violation of the natural moral law. *In other words,* the evidence that one man's power to obtain, hold, use or, in general, act, cannot be resisted or interfered with by another except at the price of moral evil on that other's part serves to influence that other to avoid such resistance or interference. Hence the power given by nature to one to influence others for his own protection or advantage is not only a *Moral* power—but also a power that can be properly called *Inviolable,* i.e., it is a power that puts a bond upon others' free will and a bond which cannot be broken by these others without *violation of natural moral law* on their part.

Q. 26.—What is the name given to such a Moral Inviolable Power to do, hold or possess certain things as one's own or to exact certain things or actions from others?

A. 26.—It is called a *Right.*

Q. 27.—Are there then such things as true rights altogether independent of and antecedent to all *positive* law?

A. 27.—There are. However, just as *Positive* Law is needed to supplement Natural Law, so positive rights may be *added* by positive law to natural rights.

Q. 28.—What are the chief points to be emphasized with regard to Rights?

A. 28.—They are as follows:

(1) The *subject* of a right, i.e., the one possessing the moral power—can be *only* a *Person;*

(2) The *matter* of a right, i.e., that which one may use or hold as one's own—can *never* be a *Person;*

(3) The *proximate* foundation of every right actually possessed by a definite person is some *fact* (either the fact of existence or some other contingent, historical fact, involving for the most part some exercise of man's activity) which establishes—in virtue of moral law—*ultimately* always the *natural* law—the actual connection between the particular person and the particular moral power. This *fact* is called the *Title* of the Right.

(4) *Some* rights are such as to be *inalienable,* i.e., they cannot be renounced or transferred to another by their possessor because the latter needs them as indispensable means to the fulfilment of duties he cannot rid himself of.

(5) Some rights have as their *essential property* the further right to use physical force in their protection—but neither the actual use of physical force nor the right to use it constitutes the *essence* of a right.

(6) To every person's right there corresponds in every other person the negative duty of non-interference and frequently in some other person or persons an affirmative duty of some kind.

(7) A *true conflict* of concrete rights is impossible, and in *seeming* conflict the stronger right, viz., that which springs from a higher or more imperative duty in the subject of the right, prevails.

With Eeclesiastical Approbation.

INDEX*

---

* References are to paragraphs.